Michi's Memories

Michi's Memories
THE STORY OF A JAPANESE WAR BRIDE

~

Keiko Tamura

Published by ANU E Press
The Australian National University
Canberra ACT 0200, Australia
Email: anuepress@anu.edu.au

This title is also available online at: http://epress.anu.edu.au

---

National Library of Australia Cataloguing-in-Publication entry

Author: Keiko Tamura

Title: Michi's memories : the story of a Japanese war bride / Keiko Tamura

ISBN: 9781921862519 (pbk.) 9781921862526 (eBook)

Notes: Includes bibliographical references.

Subjects:
    War brides — Australia.
    Japanese — Australia.
    Interracial marriage — Australia.
    Women immigrants — Australia.:

All rights reserved. No part of this publication may be reproduced, stored in a retrieval system or transmitted in any form or by any means, electronic, mechanical, photocopying or otherwise, without the prior permission of the publisher.

Originally published by Pandanus Books, 2001.

This edition © 2011 ANU E Press

"If we want to tell our story, we must call ourselves 'war brides', not just 'internationally married women'. Our unique experience in the past forty years in Japan and Australia has been the experience of war brides, not just of women who had married foreigners."

Mrs Teruko Blair in an interview with the author

Acknowledgements

MANY PEOPLE have helped make this book possible. The greatest debt is of course to Michi herself. Without her cooperation and enthusiasm, the interviews and this book production would not have been possible. From the first time I met her, Michi has been always encouraging and supportive of this project. During my research, her warm hospitality in Adelaide was most appreciated. I would also like to thank Michi's family for their understanding and cooperation. They supported this book project right from the start and Sumiko, George, Frances and William agreed to be interviewed by me. I hope this book will be of value to the present and future generations of her family, to appreciate their unique place in the history of post-war Australia.

I would like to express my deep and sincere appreciation to other Japanese war brides who were generous in their support and encouragement. They include Mrs Teruko Blair, Mrs Chiaki Foster, Mrs Sadako Morris and Mrs Kazuko Stout.

The original research for this book was carried out for my PhD thesis at the Department of Archaeology and Anthropology in The Australian National University. The thesis was submitted in August 1999 with the title "Border Crossings: Japanese War Brides and their Selfhood". During my thesis writing years, many people were helpful. Special mention needs to be made of Dr Nicolas Peterson and Professor Hank Nelson, whose continuous guidance and encouragement were invaluable throughout those years.

While I was working on this book, I was a Postdoctoral Fellow in the Division of Pacific and Asian History of the Research School of Pacific and Asian Studies at The Australian National University. Encouragement given by academic and administrative staff of the Division kept my enthusiasm going. Professor Hank Nelson and Ms Dorothy McIntosh were always ready to give me excellent advice. I am much indebted to Ms Maxine McArthur, Divisional research assistant and established writer, for her help in editing the manuscript and giving me reassurance in times of doubt and insecurity.

Publication of the book was made possible by a grant from the Ministry of Foreign Affairs of Japan. This grant was coordinated by the Embassy of Japan in Canberra. I appreciate the contribution. I hope this book will play a small role in promoting better understanding between Japan and Australia at a grass-roots level.

Finally, I thank my husband, David, and our two sons, Yoshio and Kenji, for their support and patience during the time I worked on the book. Without their understanding and encouragement, this book could never have been completed. I would like to dedicate this book to them.

Keiko Tamura
Canberra, January 2001

Contents

Acknowledgements	vii
Prologue	xi
Chapter 1 Encounters in Occupied Japan	1
Chapter 2 Marrying an Australian Soldier	15
Chapter 3 Becoming an Australian Wife and Mother	29
Chapter 4 Later Years	51
Chapter 5 Children's Views	73
Epilogue Personal Reflections	87
Endnotes	95
Selected References	98
About the Author	101

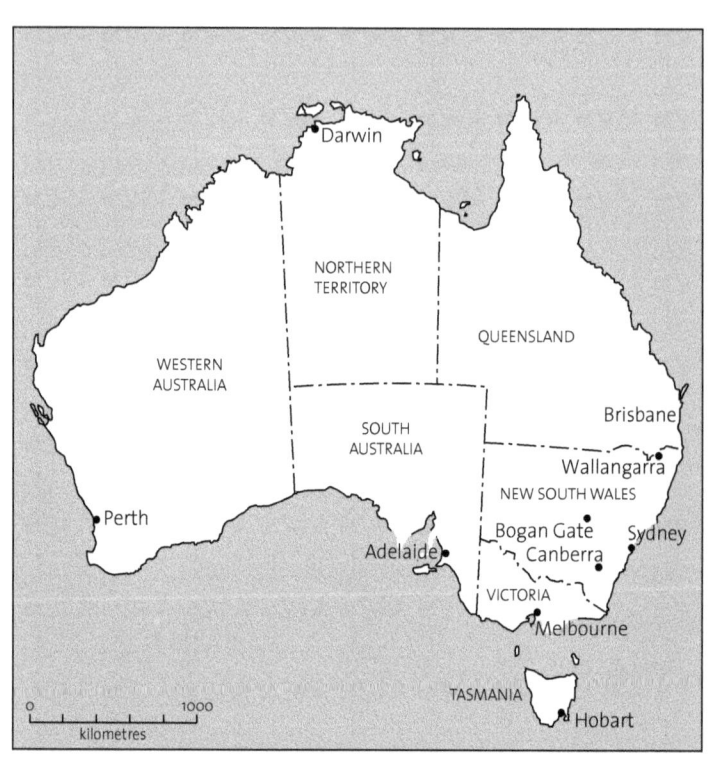

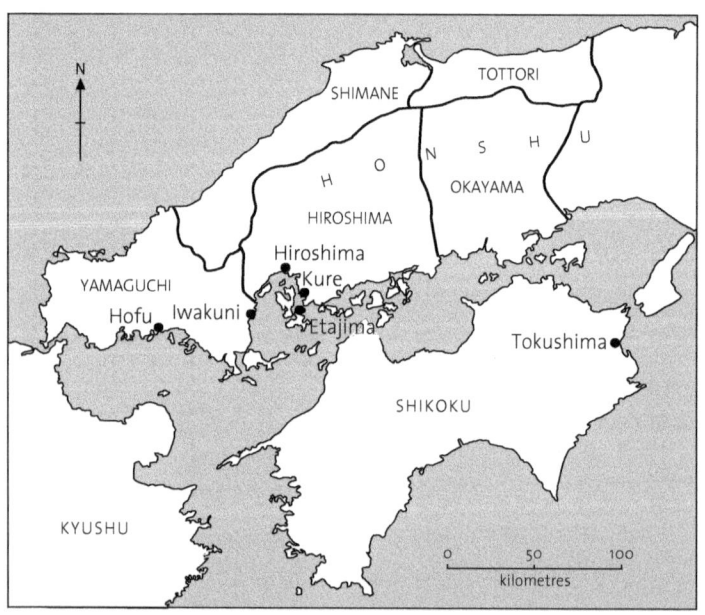

Prologue

THIS BOOK tells the story of Michi, one of 650 Japanese war brides who arrived in Australia in the early 1950s. The women met Australian servicemen in post-war Japan and decided to migrate to Australia as wives and fiancées to start a new life. In 1953, when Michi reached Sydney Harbour by boat with her two Japanese-born children, she knew only one person in Australia: her husband. She did not know any English so she quickly learned her first English phrase, "I like Australia", in the car on the way from the harbour to meet her Australian family. In the last fifty years, she brought up seven children while the family moved from one part of Australia to another. Now, in her eighties, she leads a peaceful life in Adelaide, but remains active in many ways. Her voice is full of life and she looks and sounds much younger than her age.

I met Michi for the first time in 1993 in Melbourne, at the first Japanese war bride convention in Australia. She was attending the convention with her friends from Adelaide. The day after the convention, some of the interstate participants including myself went on an excursion, and she sat across the aisle from me in the coach. In the coach, she was dozing off most of the time, probably because she had stayed up late the night before, catching up with her friends. At that time, she seemed no more than an ordinary old lady who tended to nod off frequently in moving vehicles. After the excursion, I was invited for dinner at the house where Michi was staying, so we went there together in the same car. To my surprise, as soon as we got into the car she started to tell me about her experiences in New Guinea during the war. Until then, I had not known that young women were dispatched from Japan as far as New Guinea as civilian support staff for the military during the Pacific war.

During the evening, Michi talked about her life to me and the other women who gathered there. The image I had of a sleepy old lady suddenly transformed into that of an interesting woman who had experienced so much in various parts of the world. Soon after I returned to Canberra, Michi sent me her hand-written essay in Japanese with the English title, "Life Story of an Aging War Bride", which told of her life with her Australian husband. It was a frank and moving account of her marriage and family, and further attracted my attention to her experience. I kept in touch with her by mail and met her again in Hawaii in 1994 when the first international war bride convention was held, but I could not arrange a substantial interview for a while. Finally, I travelled to Adelaide in February 1995 to interview her and other war brides in the area. I stayed at her house and carried out formal and informal interviews. I also had a chance to meet her first-born daughter, Sumiko. After the first series of interviews, I kept in regular contact with her and met her several times. The latest interview session I held was in November 1999, a month before her eightieth birthday. All the interviews were carried out in Japanese. The taped interviews were transcribed in Japanese and later translated into English by the author. The life history in this book is rendered from those interviews, informal talks and correspondence.

Michi's narrative of her experience spans over sixty years, and spans the Pacific Ocean. As an ambitious and adventurous young woman who grew up in pre-war Japan, her life changed its course dramatically during and after the Pacific War. In the face of total war and the subsequent defeat of Japan, an individual was powerless to change the political direction and social situation. For Michi, there was no choice but to follow the flow of the historical current and see where it would take her. However, as you will read in this book, there were some decisions that she made for herself and those decisions altered the course of her life. Readers will make a journey with her in time and space as she faces historical changes and personal challenges.

The original research for this book was carried out between 1993 and 1998 for my PhD thesis in Anthropology at The Australian National University, Canberra. When an opportunity to work on a book of Japanese war brides arose, I chose to tell of their experiences by focusing on Michi's life history. Since she was the eldest of all the women I interviewed, she had reached adulthood before the war started. Thus, her experience before and during the war was more dramatic compared with younger war brides who were still at school in that period. Subsequently, I organised additional interviews with Michi and her children in order to collect more information to supplement the narratives that were recorded in the initial sessions. The chapter on her children's perceptions was written for this book after interviewing the children.

I chose Michi's life history not because it was typical or representative of all the Japanese war brides in Australia. Each woman's experience is unique and it is almost impossible to generalise the experience of war brides. As the personal circumstances in which each woman found herself were different, the decisions she made and the directions she took were also different. However, there were some factors that were common among the women. The historical period they all lived through in Japan and Australia was the same. Similarly, their life course in general involved marriage, children and migration. There were some war brides who were blessed with happy marriages and financial stability all through their lives, and they might feel their stories should be told rather than the one I chose to write in this book. Michi's story was chosen because her frank narratives of her experiences and emotions moved me. I hope it will have the same impact upon readers.

For my research, I recorded twelve life history interviews, including Michi's. The shortest one was four hours and the longest seventeen hours. My taped interviews with Michi lasted over twelve hours and their transcripts covered many pages. I was grateful the women spent many exhausting hours with me. I was fortunate to have access to substantial amounts of information through the women's narratives, partly due to the friendly and trusting relationship that I managed to build up with most of the women I interviewed. At the same time, the timing of my research played an important role. By the early 1990s, the women were in their mid to late sixties, and many of them were widows. If they wanted to, they could afford to talk for hours with a researcher without worrying about working for wages or looking after their families. Furthermore, my research coincided with the time when the network among the women was established and domestic and international conventions had started to take place. It was a very interesting time for them as well as for me because we could talk not only about the past but also about present developments. Furthermore, those conventions provided me with valuable opportunities to mix with a large number of war brides and carry out participant observation.

As readers will see in the following chapters, Michi opened her heart, perhaps for the first time, and narrated her past experience. I was often surprised how frankly she talked about difficult and emotional subjects in her private life. On some occasions, memories of the past overwhelmed her and she became distressed. However, such a surge of emotion did not seem to deter her from narrating her story. I was also aware, from my experience of interviews with other women, that some issues might have been consciously omitted from her narrative. Yet, historical facts in her life history, especially her experience during the war, were checked against available historical documents in order to confirm the accuracy of her narrative. I acknowledge that each of us has some part of ourselves which we do not want to expose to others and that privacy needs to be respected. Furthermore, when one narrates a life history, one tries to tell a story with cohesiveness. Often those points that are omitted could disturb the chosen cohesiveness of the story. I believe my task in this book is to tell Michi's story in the way she wanted to tell it.

Fortunately, I have developed warm friendships with many of the war brides, including Michi. This helped me to obtain frank appraisals of their lives and to gather follow-up information. Some of them disclosed their private thoughts and intimate incidents because they developed trust in me even though they were fully aware that the interviews were carried out for research purposes. But the friendships also carry obligations towards the women. I might feel obliged to refrain from disclosing some significant information in order not to cause any subsequent embarrassment to the women. In return for their trust and friendship, I am bound by a certain level of constraint. As a researcher, I have attempted to present the information I acquired as ethically as possible.

Who are war brides?

The term "war bride" most likely originated in World War I when British servicemen stationed in France married French women. Australian servicemen who were stationed in Europe also brought back "war brides" from Britain and France around the same time. However, the largest migration of women as war brides happened during and after World War II. The biggest intake was in the United States where thousands of women arrived as war brides from allied countries, such as Britain, Australia and New Zealand, as well as from ex-enemy countries, such as Germany, Italy and Japan. Thousands of Japanese women moved to the United States as war brides, but the migration of Japanese war brides was not limited just to the United States. Michi was one of those war brides who moved from Japan to Australia.

In this book, a war bride is defined as a Japanese woman who married a member of the foreign armed forces or a foreign civilian who was in Japan as a result of the military occupation after World War II and the subsequent military presence in Japan up to 1960.

The women are generally called "*sensō hanayome*" in Japanese as the phrase is a literal translation of the English term "war bride". Since marriages between Japanese women and foreign soldiers happened only after the Pacific War, the Japanese term "*sensō hanayome*" is specifically used for those women who left Japan for their husbands' countries after World War II. It is estimated that about 50,000 women migrated to the United States and 650 to Australia. Although the numbers are not known, Japanese women also moved to Canada and the United Kingdom as well as to New Zealand as war brides.

The first chapter gives the historical background to the meeting of Japanese women and Australian servicemen in occupied Japan where interaction between the two groups was severely restricted. In this chapter, I will examine the circumstances of their encounters and analyse how their relationships were perceived then. In the following three chapters, readers will meet Michi as she narrates her life history. I divided the life history into three segments. In Chapter 2 we read of her life in Japan during and after the war, until the time of her migration to Australia. Chapter 3 tells of her experience in Australia during her family-raising years. She talks about her recent years, and her reflections on her past experiences in Chapter 4. In Chapter 5, the views of Michi's children on their mother's experience will be presented and discussed. Particular focus will be given to her eldest daughter's view. In the Epilogue, I will reflect upon war brides' lives and experiences both as a researcher, and from a personal point of view.

Chapter One
Encounters in Occupied Japan

AUSTRALIAN MEN and Japanese women who would ultimately marry in the post-war period grew up in communities and nations where people simply could not have imagined the circumstances that would lead to those marriages. Japanese society in the 1930s was becoming more militaristic and the people were growing more confident since the Japanese had no experience of defeat in wars against outside powers. At the same time, Japan was in the process of expanding its colonial power in Asia and hostility towards Britain and the United States was growing stronger among the people. Australians who grew up in the 1930s lived in a country that was over ninety per cent British by birth or descent, an amazing homogeneity for a settler nation. The White Australia Policy was strictly enforced and fear of invasions by Asian hordes was high. The Japanese were popularly seen as quaint, copiers, and toy makers but also as numerous and aggressive.

Intermarriage across the racial boundary was rare in both countries. The number of Westerners in Japan was very small and their residential areas were fairly limited, although there were some cases where Japanese women married elite Westerners who were working in Japan. Similarly, there were some intermarriages between Europeans and Asians in Australia, but the number was limited. Furthermore, inter-racial marriages were seen with prejudice and regarded as problematic. Thus, intimate relationships which eventually occurred and subsequent requests for marriages between Australian soldiers and Japanese women were received with shock and hostility in both countries.

2 Overview of the Australian presence in Japan

After Japan surrendered in August 1945, the country was occupied by Allied Forces until the Peace Treaty was signed in 1951. The first forces to arrive in Japan in September were more than 430,000 American GIs. They were scattered in each prefecture in Japan in order to control the population of 70 million. Australia's role in the occupation was in the western part of Japan as a member of the British Commonwealth Occupation Forces (BCOF), which consisted of troops from four nations: Britain, Australia, New Zealand and India. The BCOF servicemen started to arrive in Japan in February 1946, and they totalled just over 37,000 at the end of the year. Of these, approximately 11,000 were Australians, who outnumbered the troops from any other nation, and played the major role in the occupation. Australia's responsibility was for Hiroshima Prefecture and most of the Australian contingent were stationed around Kure, about forty kilometres east of the city of Hiroshima, which was devastated by the atomic bomb.

Until the end of the war, Kure had been one of the four major Japanese Navy bases and boasted not only one of the most advanced shipbuilding yards, but also aircraft factories.[1] The buildings of the naval cadet school to train future naval officers stood proudly on Eta-jima, an island off Kure. Thus, the working population of Kure was an interesting mixture of career military servicemen, sailors, engineers, technicians and factory workers, all of whom were fiercely proud of the Japanese Navy tradition. The town, however, received severe damage from a series of Allied air raids, and the breaking up of the Imperial Navy resulted in a sharp population decline from 400,000 to 150,000. When the Australian soldiers arrived by boat in February 1946, their first sight was of the port, littered with sunken naval vessels, and the burnt-out town with shacks and starving people.

The main duties of the BCOF were to disarm the Japanese forces and demilitarise depots and various establishments in the occupied areas. Many members of the Australian contingent were fresh young volunteers who had not been old enough to fight during the war. For most of them, joining BCOF provided them with the chance to go overseas — something they had missed during the war. Others in the contingent had found it difficult to settle down to civilian life after the war. Although there were some exceptions, it is fair to say the majority of the soldiers in the Australian contingent were young and restless and looking for some type of adventure. Soon after their arrival, however, the BCOF soldiers found out that there was virtually no resistance from Japanese forces or the general Japanese population to the occupation forces. Thus, the occupying soldiers' main task was to demilitarise naval facilities in Kure port and supervise the democratisation process in the occupied area.

The number of Australian servicemen in Japan peaked in February 1947 at 12,000 and gradually declined as the social situation in Japan stabilised. In March 1950, when the Australian Cabinet decided to withdraw the BCOF entirely, there were only about 2,300 servicemen remaining in Japan. However, the start of the Korean War in June 1950 reversed the previous decision to withdraw, resulting in a continuation of the Australian presence in Japan. Subsequently, the number of Australian troops was increased to take part in the British Commonwealth Forces, Korea (BCFK), which itself was a part of the United Nation Forces. After the cease-fire agreement in 1953, it was inevitable that the Australians would eventually leave Japan. Scaling down of the camp followed. In November 1956, the last group of Australian servicemen left Kure and the ten-year Australian military presence in Japan came to an end.

Initial contacts of the locals with American occupation forces

The Kure area was initially occupied by the Americans for four months between October 1945 and February 1946. Before the Americans' arrival, several instructions were issued by Naval Headquarters to the local population in order to calm anxiety and to ensure order for the incoming forces. These instructions clearly indicated that the Japanese administrators were not certain what to expect of the Allied soldiers. Subsequently, the residents were discouraged from initiating any contact with members of the occupation forces. Some of the instructions read as follows (translation by Tamura):

In order to avoid misunderstandings with the arrival of many foreigners who have different customs, habits and language, the following instructions are listed.

It is important for each individual as a Japanese national to handle the situation with dignity and with pride.

Communicating with a smattering of English might cause problems, so it is better not to say anything.

Women should wear *monpe* trousers and should not expose their skin, bare feet or breasts.[2]

Women and children should not stare at, laugh at, or wave handkerchiefs at the occupation soldiers.

Do not go outside alone. Try to avoid walking outside at night.

In emergencies, ask for help by running outside or shouting loudly. Try to remember the intruder's ID numbers and any characteristics, and report to the authorities as soon as possible.

With these instructions, cards were distributed to each household. People were to show them to the soldiers when they did not know what to do. The card was written in both Japanese and English and the Japanese instruction said that "Attached card is to show to a foreigner when he trespasses into your house and demands something". The English section reads as follows:

To the Men of the Allied Troops.

The order of the General Headquarters of the Allied Forces states that all negotiations regarding buildings, houses, automobiles, etc. should be done through the Central Liaison Office and not directly by private individuals.

Americans soldiers initially anticipated that they would have to face fierce resistance from the Japanese population. However, soon after their arrival, they realised that the Japanese had no intention of carrying on the fighting. Similarly, Kure residents were relieved to learn that the occupation soldiers were not "demons and beasts" as they had been told during the war. On the contrary, many of them expressed their friendliness towards the civilian population by giving away chewing gum and chocolate to local children or organising baseball matches with Japanese residents. In contrast, the BCOF's attitude towards the Japanese was characteristically more rigid.

BCOF and anti-fraternisation policy

The war Australia fought against Japan was filled with savage and horrific experiences. The jungle warfare in New Guinea and surrounding islands was extremely difficult for the Australians not just because of geography and climate, but because of the prevalence of diseases among the soldiers. In addition, the Australian public were well informed of the atrocities inflicted by the Japanese on the Australian POWs in Rabaul, Singapore and the Thai–Burma Railway. Fresh testimonies were steadily coming out well into the 1950s during the series of war crime trials. Notions of the Japanese as a violent and cruel people were well planted in the soldiers' minds before their arrival.

Consequently, BCOF authorities believed that it was important to treat the Japanese with detachment in order to carry out their aims as an occupation force. Prior to the landing in Kure in February 1946, a brochure with the title *Your Japan* was distributed among Australian soldiers. The brochure warned the soldiers not to have high expectations in Japan, and encouraged them to detach themselves emotionally from the local population. Similarly, a pamphlet, *BCOF Bound*, which was distributed among the families of BCOF servicemen before heading for Japan in 1947, elaborated the roles of BCOF as "to represent worthily and to maintain and enhance British Commonwealth prestige and influence in the eyes of the Japanese and of our Allies, and to show to, and impress on, the Japanese, the democratic way and purpose in life".

In spite of their official stance, the Australian Army seems to have predicted that problems would arise from interaction between the Japanese public and Australian soldiers. Lieutenant General Northcott, Commander-in-Chief of BCOF, issued further instructions against fraternisation to the soldiers in March 1946, only a month after their arrival in Kure. In these instructions, each member of BCOF was reminded that "in dealing with the Japanese he is dealing with a conquered enemy who has, by making war against us, caused deep suffering and loss in many thousands of homes throughout the British Empire". A soldier was instructed that he "must be formal and correct" towards the Japanese and he "must not enter their homes or take part in their family life" and his "unofficial dealing with the Japanese must be kept to a minimum".[3]

6   Although the Army did not state it clearly, it was most likely that one of their main worries was the possibility of servicemen fraternising with Japanese women. Measures were swiftly taken to avoid the possibility of marriages between Australian servicemen and Japanese women. Specific instructions said that no member of BCOF could marry without the written authority of the Commander-in-Chief. If a marriage ceremony was carried out without permission, it stated that:

> all ranks are warned that:
>
> (a) Disciplinary action will be considered.
>
> (b) An Asiatic woman, notwithstanding her marriage to an Australian serviceman will, as a general rule, be debarred admission to Australia.
>
> (c) Dependents' and marriage allowances may in certain cases be withheld.[4]

Thus, it was made quite clear to the servicemen that marriages without permission were prohibited and that applications for permits would almost certainly be refused. If a soldier ignored the rule and married without permission, he could neither go back to Australia with his wife nor support her in Japan.

Encounters under the anti-fraternisation policy

The actual policing of the anti-fraternisation policy in occupied areas was supposed to be done by provosts (military police) who patrolled "out of bounds" areas, such as illegal brothels and other entertainment areas. However, in reality, policing was not carried out thoroughly by the BCOF authorities mainly because strict enforcement was simply impossible. As long as it was done discreetly, visiting brothels was tolerated and sexual encounters were readily available for the other ranks.

The result of all of this type of fraternisation was the spread of venereal disease among the BCOF soldiers. In spite of the effort by medical officers to warn the soldiers about infection, 286 cases of VD had occurred as early as March 1946. The incidence of VD increased rapidly and by the end of that December the number of cases had increased to

4,500, which was well above the 32 per cent of the force that made up the Australian contingent. The authorities had to make arrangements to prevent further spread of the disease in order to avoid embarrassing publicity in Australia. The authorities tried to discourage the soldiers from having casual sexual encounters by introducing various sanctions against those who caught the disease, such as confinement, reduced rations of beer, and public humiliation.

BCOF and Japanese authorities also tried to control the spread of VD by screening Japanese women. Medical checks were carried out regularly among prostitutes. When women wanted to be employed at the camp, they were obliged to take not only TB but also VD tests.[5] Furthermore, Japanese women seen in the company of Australian soldiers were often regarded as prostitutes and were taken to the police by provosts for a VD check. The procedure resulted in humiliating experiences for many innocent women in the area. However, in reality, it was not possible to enforce this policy completely and the provosts would generally turn a blind eye unless cases were serious, because they themselves often had Japanese girlfriends.

In spite of the anti-fraternisation policy, contact between BCOF servicemen and the local Japanese population was obviously close and frequent. Moreover, this contact was not limited to casual sexual encounters. In reality, contact was varied in nature and some of the encounters were genuinely friendly ones for both parties. Here I examine three types of interactions as they took place in the camp, in the black markets, and within the private sphere.

Kure residents shared their lives with Australian servicemen for almost ten years. During that period the BCOF and BCFK camps were important sources of employment for Japanese residents. At the same time, BCOF was dependent on Japanese labour in various areas of the organisation in order to run the occupation effectively. Soon after the start of the occupation, about 8,000 Japanese workers were employed by BCOF. The number of Japanese workers in Kure increased further and reached over 20,000 in October of 1946.

Initially the Kure people, who had been fiercely proud of the Imperial Naval tradition, were reluctant to search for jobs in the BCOF camp because many of them regarded working for the ex-enemy for wages as a disgrace. Fear of the unknown probably played a part in their hesitation, too. However, after the air raids and disbandment of the Navy, there were virtually no jobs in the traditional sectors and people were desperate for food and shelter. The jobs in the camp were a strong incentive for Kure people. The wages in the camp were paid at the standard of public servant jobs plus 10 per cent in the early stage of the occupation, and employees were provided with meals while they were on duty.[6] For many women, the camp offered various job opportunities: waitress, house girl, canteen worker, office worker, typist, and interpreter. The main type of employment for women was as house girls, whose duties were to clean living quarters for servicemen and families and to look after their day-to-day needs.

In addition to better wages and the provision of meals, the availability of surplus goods in the camp also attracted Japanese workers. They were occasionally given unwanted goods by their bosses as gifts or were asked to exchange them on the black market on behalf of BCOF members. However, the authorities' official position was to prohibit Japanese workers from receiving any goods from the servicemen, for fear of those goods being sold in the black market. Occasional random checks were carried out at the camp gate to see if any Japanese workers were trying to smuggle out BCOF supplies and those who were caught with the goods were fired.

Within the camp, interactions between Japanese employees and Australian servicemen were frequent and both parties retained warm memories of each other.[7] The house girls were the ones the servicemen and their families remembered most vividly due to their close and daily contact. Most of the house girls were young single women. It was inevitable that many of those interactions between the Japanese women and the Australian servicemen eventually developed into sexual relationships. As a result of battle casualties there was a serious shortage of marriageable Japanese men.[8] Consciously or unconsciously, many young Japanese women would have been aware that if they wanted to talk, dance, flirt, go on a date or have a sexual relationship with an uncommitted young man, then it would have to be with a soldier from the occupying forces.

On the other hand, some of the house girls were much older women who were married or widowed and their relationships with the soldiers were quite different from those of the younger ones. Some soldiers affectionately remembered the motherly concern and care those older women showed. These women nagged and scolded the untidy habits and drinking of those young men just as they did their own sons. Relationships between the soldiers and the domestic staff developed beyond the interaction between the victor and the defeated, or employer and employee. Clearly there were exchanges of a wide range of feelings between these two parties.

Black market activities offered the chance for both Australians and Japanese to interact during negotiations over various goods and presented a different type of interaction between the two parties. By the time the BCOF arrived in Kure, there were already open-air black markets operating in various locations in the town, where all kinds of goods were traded illegally outside the official distribution of rations. The Australian soldiers soon started to participate in these activities mainly as suppliers of goods in exchange for cash by selling off their rations of condensed milk, soap and cigarettes. Some soldiers even asked their families in Australia to send them knitting wool so that they could sell it in Japan.

In the competitive and serious atmosphere of the markets, both the Japanese and the Australians tried to outstrip each other for better deals. A soldier remembered that he shook a tin of thin condensed milk in order to sell it as a thickened one. Similarly, Japanese traders remembered that they often cheated soldiers when prices of the goods needed to be converted into pounds and shillings. They claimed that they could take advantage of some Australian soldiers in payments because the Japanese were much quicker in converting the currencies in their heads.[9] At the end, each side was convinced that they were outdoing the other and was happy with the result.

Other than in the camp and at the black markets, Australian servicemen had various occasions to meet Japanese residents in Kure and surrounding areas. Some of them met and became friendly with the local residents while they were patrolling or while they were off duty. Although the anti-fraternisation policy prohibited the soldiers from entering private houses, they soon found themselves sitting in the local residents' living rooms for goodwill visits. On those occasions, visiting was carried out without any pretentiousness on the part of the victors "to demonstrate democracy and act as a model for Japanese people". The Australian soldiers were curious and interested in different peoples and their lifestyles and there were genuinely friendly interactions. The soldiers' various accounts showed that they did not seem to care whether their conduct was against the anti-fraternisation policy or not. They mixed with the Japanese people in order to get to know them better.

The anti-fraternisation policy was supposed to be applied not only to members of the service, but to their family members as well. However, many family members gradually developed personal relationships not only with their house girls but also with other members of the Japanese community through organisations such as the YWCA and churches. After the war, with the introduction of Western values, Christianity became popular and church attendance by the Japanese increased. While American Forces redefined their fraternisation policy in 1949 and decided to relax the policy further, the Australian Government maintained its strict anti-fraternisation policy. At that time, Australian church ministers who worked in Japan were worried that the attendance of the Japanese at their church might be prohibited by the policy. The Chaplain General urged the government to allow the continuation of Japanese attendance at BCOF churches and argued that this should be permitted in accordance with the policy which stated one of the objectives of BCOF was "to illustrate to and impress on the Japanese people as far as may be possible the Democratic way and purpose in life". The response, which was classified as top secret, was relayed back and approved the continuing attendance of Japanese people in spite of the fact that in earlier correspondence the possibility of marriage between Japanese women and Australian soldiers had been suggested.

Australian servicemen's perception of Japanese women

From an early stage in the occupation, it was clear that BCOF soldiers saw Japanese women differently from Japanese men. In the pamphlet *BCOF Bound*, which was distributed to the servicemen before their arrival in Japan, it said that "The women appear to be somewhat different. It has been said that Japan is inhabited by two races, the men and the women. The women, firstly, work for their families, and exchange that on marriage for working for their husband and their children."[10] The Japanese men were assumed to be responsible for the wartime aggression by Japan, but the women were removed from this responsibility and were seen in the context of a domestic existence.

Such a perception of the two sexes in Japan seemed to have been prevalent among the Australian soldiers who were actually stationed there. An intelligence report in March 1947 said, "most troops admit of only two categories of JAPANESE — pretty girls and 'bastards'. Prolonged observation would suggest that this conception is indeed fairly widespread, especially amongst lower ranks."[11] The girls were given a general name among the soldiers: "moose". This word came from the Japanese word *musume* for unmarried girls.

Requests for marriages

It was inevitable that some associations between Australian soldiers and Japanese women would lead to more serious relationships. Eventually, in spite of the anti-fraternisation policy and the effective marriage ban, some soldiers started to explore the possibility of marriage. Applications for permission to marry started to appear soon after the start of the occupation in spite of the announcement of the marriage ban. The first application which was officially submitted to BCOF authorities was by Corporal H.J. Cooke in October 1947. In 1948, a soldier named John Henderson was sent back to Australia after he told his senior officer that he had secretly married a Japanese woman. Back in Australia, he appealed to the Returned Soldiers League to assist him to bring his wife and child back to Australia. His appeal was reported in the media, but his application for recognition of the marriage was rejected. The then Labor Government Minister of Immigration, Arthur Calwell, publicly expressed his objection to and disgust about fraternisation which led to Henderson's marriage application. He stated that "while relatives remain of the men who suffered at the hands of the Japanese, it would be the grossest act of public indecency to permit a Japanese of either sex to pollute Australian or Australian-controlled shores".

In spite of strong opposition from some sections of the government and public, more applications started to appear. Among those, Gordon Parker's plea to bring his wife, Cherry (nee Nobuko Sakuramoto), and two children to Australia was well publicised by the media. The government felt pressure to change its policy as the Peace Treaty was negotiated and trade relations with Japan seemed certain to develop. Whatever they thought about Japanese women "polluting" Australian soil, Australians certainly wanted to export wool to Japan.

In March 1952, a month before the Peace Treaty officially became effective, Japanese women who were married to Australian soldiers were permitted to enter Australia by Harold Holt, who had replaced Calwell as Minister of Immigration due to the election of the new Menzies government. Originally, Holt expected the number of women who would seek entry to Australia to be around a dozen. However, a much larger number of soldiers started to place their applications. After Cherry Parker's arrival in Australia as the first Japanese war bride in June 1952 was well received in the media, the number of applications increased dramatically. By the time the Australian presence in Japan ended in November 1956, about 650 women had migrated to Australia as wives and fiancées of Australian soldiers.[12]

Bringing the brides home

The actual process of granting official permission for Australian servicemen to marry Japanese women has not been well documented. However, according to the oral accounts I have collected, cautious and often discouraging attitudes towards marriage applications were evidenced by the authorities. Numerous forms needed to be submitted to the military authorities in order to obtain permission to marry and bring a Japanese wife back to Australia. In addition to this documentation, the wives had to have thorough medical and character checks.

After an application for marriage was lodged by a soldier, an officer usually made an informal inquiry to the sergeant major about the applicant's personality and seriousness of his intention. Subsequently, he explained to the applicant the implications of bringing a Japanese wife to Australia when hostility toward Japan was still strong among the general public. At the same time, a character check was done on the woman and her family by the Japanese police. The neighbours of the family were visited by the police and interviewed in order to confirm that the woman was socially respectable and not an opportunist who wanted to marry an Australian just to get out of the country. They also checked whether any of the family members were engaging in communist activities. When the background research proved the woman to be acceptable, she was interviewed by a senior officer with an interpreter in order to find out whether she was "genuine".

In those interviews, officers explained cultural differences between Australia and Japan and tried to convey realistic pictures of life in Australia. A senior officer who interviewed those women told me that some women had rather too "glamorous" views of Australia with "flash cars and flush toilets". However, he also remembered most of the women were fairly practical and were merely "looking for a better life after a hard life in Japan during the war". The women were interested in finding out more information on the Australian way of life and asked him questions regarding food, cooking, schooling and fashion.[13] When those interviews concluded successfully, permission to marry was granted by the Army.

In order to prepare the Japanese women for their new life, the Australian Army established a bride school within the camp in Kure in January 1953. The lectures were given through interpreters by Australian staff who worked in the YWCA. Miss Nell Stronach, one of the teachers, said that the women were taught "shopping conditions, western hygiene, the wearing of western clothes and cooking" in the classes. Some women remembered learning to cook chops and Irish stews and to dress in the Australian fashion.

The departure of the Japanese war brides to Australia started in June 1952 when the first bride, Cherry Parker, left Japan. Larger numbers of the women started to migrate to Australia in the next year and there were several "bride ships" organised for those war brides whose husbands or fiancés were still in the military services. A few boats in early 1953 carried more than thirty women as well as their children from Japan to Australia.

Women who were left behind

By the time the Australian military presence ended in November 1956, several hundred women had migrated to Australia. At the same time, many women who had relationships with Australian servicemen were left behind in Japan. Most of them had been hoping to join their husbands and boyfriends in Australia, but never heard the good news from Australia. Some decided not to leave Japan mainly because of their responsibility to their own families. In the end, they had to re-establish their lives on their own in Japan. It is impossible to estimate the number of those women, but the number of children whose fathers were identified as Australians was known. According to a survey carried out by the International Social Service of Japan in 1959, there were 52 children whose fathers were Australian servicemen living in the Kure area. Most of those children had to face enormous difficulties in the society where they grew up. Their mothers often had serious economic problems in caring for the children by themselves, and some left the children with their grandparents to be brought up. Furthermore, the fact that they were mixed-blood and that their fathers had left them cast a strong social stigma on those children.[14]

From the foregoing, it is clear that the interactions between Japanese people and Australian servicemen were frequent and close, even though an anti-fraternisation policy was enforced officially by the BCOF. Some intimate and serious relationships between Japanese women and Australian soldiers emerged, not as exceptions, but as a natural progression of the interaction between those two parties. However, the feelings between them were not readily welcomed by the authorities and they had to cross several hurdles before the women were admitted to Australia as brides of Australian servicemen. In the next chapter, the first section of Michi's life history will be presented. She narrates what it was like to live through the period of the war and occupation, and tells how she made up her mind to marry an Australian soldier. Her narrative also reveals how her family reacted to this unconventional decision.

Chapter Two
Marrying an Australian Soldier

THIS CHAPTER covers Michi's experience from her childhood in the Japanese countryside to the early 1950s when she left Japan for Australia. During that period, many drastic changes took place in Japan. Japan was virtually at war with China from 1937 with the aspiration of expanding its colonial power. The Pacific War started in 1941 and, by the time Japan was defeated in 1945, 2.6 million houses were burnt in air raids and 13 million people were homeless in Japan. The defeat also signalled the arrival of occupation soldiers; among those was an Australian soldier whom Michi eventually married.

Michi's story

I was born on 30 December in 1919 as Ayako Yoshida in Tokushima Prefecture on Shikoku Island as the eldest child of eight. I had two younger brothers and five younger sisters. My father was a wealthy landowner of fields and mountains in a farming village. I heard that the family used to run an indigo dye production business, indigo dye being a well-known local product in Tokushima area. My mother's family was from the *samurai* line who used to serve as high-ranking advisers for the Hachisuka family who were the lords in the area, so she was brought up with strict discipline. She was a high school graduate and was better educated than my father who had compulsory education only. She was respected as a women's leader in the community and served as a head of the local *Kokubō Fujinkai* branch [National Defence Women's Association] before and during the war. I heard I was a very religious girl since I was small. I used to visit local shrines often to make wishes.

Michi (back, right) in her uniform with her office mates when she was working as an office assistant. Two girls in front in kimono were working as kitchen hands. The photo was taken on a balcony of the Asahi Newspaper building in Osaka.

Later, when I moved to Tokyo, I visited Yasukuni Shrine and Meiji Shrine quite often. Maybe the reason I joined Sōka Gakkai later in my life had something to do with this temperament.

We had a big problem at home. My father indulged in drink and women and wasted the family's wealth for his own pleasure. My mother had to endure all the financial problems and cope with a series of young women my father had relationships with. As the eldest child in the family, I felt responsible for the family and wanted to do something. However, at the same time, I did not like watching my father act selfishly and seeing my mother suffer and cry. I felt sorry for my mother and disgusted with my father. But, at the same time, I could not do anything to improve the situation for my mother.

After I finished my schooling, I stayed in Tokushima for three years while I learned sewing kimonos, but then I left home for Osaka to look for a job. I was about 15 years old. It was more like a revolt against my father. I just did not want to be in the same house with him. My mother did not want me to go, probably because she wanted to have somebody to support her emotionally. My father was not around much at home then, so I did not ask for his permission. Initially, I stayed with my relatives in Osaka. Luckily, I was able to find a job in the local news section at the Asahi Newspaper as a junior office assistant. My job was to serve tea to the staff and do odd jobs for them, but I also had the chance to mix with journalists. I started to have an interest in writing and wrote a few essays for myself. I also met several reporters from the Asahi's Tokyo office. As they told me about Tokyo, I began to dream of moving there because Tokyo seemed such an exciting city.

In 1938, I did shift to Tokyo. I was 19 years old then. After I arrived in the city, I applied for a job at the Asahi office there and told them that I was working in the Osaka branch of the newspaper. Luckily I was offered the same type of job that I used to do in Osaka. At the office, there were opportunities to learn other types of jobs and I started to work more in the reporting department. In addition, there was a chance to learn film production in Asahi News Films. I received training as a sound engineer for newsreels, adding the sound of artillery and guns to the film. Other training I received included editing films. One of my works was a short

Michi in her early twenties when she was working for Asahi Film in Tokyo. She was taking evening courses in English and Japanese typing around this period.

film, *Jack and the Bean Stalk*, and I felt very proud to see my name in the credits. I felt ambitious and wanted to become a film director for a while. However, soon I realised how difficult it was to master various skills in film production after I actually started to work in the industry. So I accepted the fact that I probably would not go any further than editing in the profession.

When I was in Tokyo, I met a university student. His family name was Shibayama. Although it was difficult to date openly around that time, we became very close and fell in love. The general atmosphere in society was getting more and more tense as the war approached. People frowned upon anybody who was having a good time, so you dared not date openly nor walk with your boyfriend. Yet, we managed to see each other quite often. Eventually, we got engaged but kept it secret because we could not expect his family to be happy with our marriage. He came from an academic family. His grandfather was president of a university in Kyoto and his mother was a graduate of a prestigious women's teaching college in Nara. On the other hand, I came from a farming family in the countryside and my father had been wasting away our estate on drinks and women. It was clear that the difference between those two families was too great. We started to live together and contemplated emigrating overseas so that we could marry in spite of his family's opposition. Then the war started and my fiancé was conscripted into the Navy as an officer and was going to be sent to New Guinea in the paymaster section. I heard that the Civilian Section of the Navy was looking for female staff who would work in New Guinea. I decided to volunteer for the Navy as a civilian worker and received training as a typist for three or four months. Luckily, both of us were posted to the same place, Manokwari in Dutch New Guinea, in 1943. I think he was sent there earlier by plane. I was in the Second Dispatchment of the Navy Civil Government and left Kobe on a big cargo boat to New Guinea.

After occupying Dutch New Guinea in April 1942, the Japanese Navy decided to establish a civilian government in the occupied territory. The headquarters was to be established in Manokwari. In Tokyo, the staff of the newly established New Guinea Civil Government, which numbered 500, was assembled to make preparation for the dispatchment. About thirty female staff who were typists and nurses were included. In addition to the government staff, sixteen trading companies decided to send a total of 2,100 employees to

New Guinea to join the government staff. In addition to the staff who worked for the public and private sectors, there were 200 university and company researchers whose task was to survey the area. Thus, a total of 2,800 Japanese were divided into two groups and left Japan by boat. The first group arrived in Manokwari in February 1943 and the second group in April. The original aim of the civil government was to explore rich resources in Dutch New Guinea and to develop industries such as paper mills in the area.

Japan was winning the war then and we went to New Guinea with the advancing forces. In Manokwari, Shibayama and I could spend some time together. Since he was a navy officer and I was a civilian worker, the difference in ranks was big. We could not show our closeness too much, but people knew that we were planning to get married. We could see each other after work. When one of us got ill, dengue fever in his case and malaria in my case, we looked after each other. We were happy to be in the same place at the same time.

There were some other women in Manokwari who were posted there as civilian workers. Some of them were nurses and others were typists like myself. There were also many male civilian workers who were dispatched there to carry out construction and logging. All of us lived in the same compound and got together at assemblies at seven o'clock in the morning. The Japanese flag was hoisted up the flagpole with the sound of a bugle at the assemblies. We lived in quarters that were previously occupied by Dutch officers. The houses were concrete buildings and well equipped. They even had water closets.

The reason I volunteered to become a civilian worker in New Guinea was not solely because I wanted to follow Shibayama. When I look back I realised that it was quite an adventure to go to New Guinea as a civilian worker, but at that time, I did not feel scared because there were other people, including women, who were going there. If my father had been decent and had not womanised too much, I might have stayed at home quietly without venturing into those things. But I feel I always had an adventurous spirit. That is why I am here in Australia now. Through my work at the Asahi, I met many journalists who worked as war correspondents and they told me of their experiences overseas. I also met Fumiko Hayashi, a well-known female novelist, when she visited our office. I took her around the building and explained to her about film production. She asked me about my background and when she realised I was originally from Tokushima, she urged me to visit Onomichi where she came from because these two districts were relatively close. Since she was very famous then, I was so happy to have a chance to talk to her in person. The last time I saw her, she was off to Indochina as a war correspondent. She was wearing a military cap and saying goodbye to well-wishers at Tokyo Station. I also heard a rumour that the Asahi Film might close down soon as it would be amalgamated with other news production companies. Then I might lose my job at the Asahi Film. I was still young then, and wanted to go overseas. Around that time, the Navy established the civilian governing section in New Guinea and advertised for staff.

We could sense the deterioration of the war, being in Manokwari. By 1944, Japan started to lose the war and Manokwari was bombed heavily. Young pilots with white scarves started to arrive as members of Tokkō-tai (Kamikaze Squad). Those pilots were to steer their planes to the target while they remained in the cockpits. At farewells before their sorties, I was asked by Shibayama to pour some sake in their glasses. One young pilot declined and I asked him why. He said he could not drink. He was only seventeen years old then. I felt so sad and tears started to trickle down my face. Their planes left the airstrip whenever the planes could secure enough fuel, but none of us expected them to return.

In one air raid in Manokwari, we were evacuated to a bomb shelter. My colleague who was sitting next to me offered to swap places and the next moment, a bomb hit the shelter. The colleague who was sitting in the position where I had been a moment before was killed instantly. I felt sorry for him, but I also felt very lucky. I really felt I was given strong luck and strength to survive then.

Eventually, we were ordered to evacuate Manokwari and we had to return to Japan by boat. At the same time, Shibayama was also about to leave for Ambon. During the trip back to Japan, our boat was followed by a submarine which tried to torpedo us. The boat had to weave to left and right in order to evade the torpedos. I was totally terrified. I thought the end had come for us. During this ordeal, I was in a cabin where bones of dead soldiers were stored in order to send them back to Japan. I clutched at a wooden box of bones as the fear was overwhelming me. The grinding sound of the boat while it was changing its course at full speed was something I could not forget. When I realised that we survived the attack, the box which I had been holding was almost shattered in my arms. Another boat in our convoy was not as lucky as ours. It was hit by torpedoes and sank in a very short time. While the ship was going down, its siren was going off all through it. Somebody must have been blowing the siren in the sinking boat. It was such a dreary sound and I can still remember it clearly. When we stopped in Manila, I saw a woman's body floating in the harbour. Initially, I thought she was clutching onto something, then I realised that her lower half was missing, probably eaten by a shark. It was such a shocking sight. When we finally reached Tokyo unharmed, I really felt I had strong luck then.

As Michi narrated, soon after the Japanese arrived in the area in 1943, the bombing by the Allies became more intense. By May, the Japanese needed to put their energy into digging air raid shelters instead of developing new industries. Some of the female staff left Manokwari for Japan in October 1943. As the situation in Eastern New Guinea became more serious for Japan, the Civil Government in New Guinea was disbanded in February 1944 and the rest of the women, including Michi, and sick staff were sent back to Japan in April 1944. Eventually, towards the end of the war, some of the staff in Manokwari retreated to Ambon. The rest remained in the area and tried to support themselves by growing their own food as their supply was cut. After the end of the Pacific War, those who remained in Manokwari and the rest who retreated to Ambon were repatriated to Japan in June 1946.

Back in Tokyo, I went to visit Shibayama's mother. She had been living alone since both of her two sons were sent overseas in the war. Shibayama had written letters to his mother about me from Manokwari and informed her that I would come and visit her when I arrived back in Japan. So it was not a complete surprise for her to receive me. As she was living on her own, she asked if I could stay with her. We experienced air raids but were not burned out because her house was not near the centre of the city. Eventually, we heard that Shibayama was sent to Ambon from Manokwari. We received a letter from him from Ambon, but we heard that he was killed there sometime later. Of course I was shocked to hear his death, but I told myself that I was not the only one who was separated from a loved one by death. Some of my friends were left behind with children. A husband of my friend was killed in the war and she and her three children lived with his parents after the war. She had a hard time looking after her parents-in-law as well as her own children. So I consoled myself by saying that I needed to look after myself only and I was in a better position than some of my friends.

I found a job at a department store in Tokyo as a typist after the war. The situation in the city was awfully depressing. I saw hordes of orphans who wore only rags and lived on the streets and around the Ueno Station Underpass. I deplored the situation Japan found itself in. When I saw a child who was barely three years of age walk with another younger one in hand, I felt too depressed to cry. I could not help them in any way because I hardly had any extra means other than looking after my own welfare. What Japan is now must have been created by that generation of those children and those returned soldiers who were starving. I really appreciate their contribution to Japan. On the other hand, I did not do anything because I left Japan for Australia soon after that.

While I was working at the department store, I was summoned by the GHQ. The GHQ found my name on the list of typists in the Philippines and I was taken to the Sugamo Prison to be interrogated. In addition, occupation soldiers visited my parents' house in Tokushima and seized towels and a bar of soap that I brought back from overseas for my parents. Although they did not find anything suspicious about me, this incident really scared me. Shibayama's mother wanted to move to Nara to be with her own family as her second son was sent from China to Siberia and detained there. He was sent there from China by the Soviet Army and I do not know when he actually came back to Japan. There was nothing to keep me in Tokyo, so I decided to go back to Tokushima.

In Tokushima, I started to work in a local branch of Asahi Newspaper as an assistant editor, checking articles to see if any of them violated censorship which the occupation forces had enforced. That was where I met Gus. His real name was Angus, but everybody called him Gus. He came to check ammunition stored in Wadajima by the Japanese military and visited the Asahi branch. At that time, I was asked to look after him and his colleagues because the newspaper staff thought I could speak English. They thought I could speak English because I was in New Guinea during the war, but, in reality, I could not. Gus had learned some Japanese and could speak the language a little. His smattering of Japanese sounded rather charming to me. After the first

Michi when she was taking dance lessons in Okayama around the time she met Gus.

visit, he came to the office whenever he visited Wadajima. Soon he said he could not visit the island anymore and had to move to Okayama because of a transfer. I went and visited him once or twice a month in Okayama. Of course, I did not tell my parents about Gus. I always told them that I was going to see my girlfriend in Okayama. He would usually write me a letter in *katakana* [Japanese phonetic symbols] and tell me where we should meet. We usually met at a station and spent our time at an inn. Eventually, we decided to rent a house in Okayama and I moved in. In the meantime, I resigned from the Asahi. When he was transferred to Kure, I followed him. We rented a house there and Sumiko, my daughter, was born in Kirikushi near Kure. Gus became a father when he was only twenty-one. He did not know I was seven years older than him! He never asked my age!

I really enjoyed the time I was dating Gus. During the war, we had a hard time. With Shibayama in Tokyo, I could not date openly because the atmosphere was very tense. After the war, food was scarce and life was tough. I sometimes felt self-conscious dating a foreigner, but there were many couples like us, so we were not completely odd ones out. We still could not walk on the street hand in hand. The Military Police patrolled the area and arrested those who were fraternising. I was really scared of the Military Police because I was not sure where they would take me. We could not see each other so often. Probably once or twice a month at the most. To be frank, one of the reasons why young Japanese women wanted to be with those occupation soldiers was that there were not enough young Japanese men for us then. Also the Australian soldiers were open and happy and enjoying themselves. In contrast, Japanese men seemed to be dragging dark shadows with them. Occupation soldiers also had money. No wonder many women felt attracted to those men. I was aware of the hostility people felt towards the women who were walking with the occupation soldiers. People did not bother to distinguish those ordinary girls from prostitutes and categorised all of us as call girls. They used to call those who lived with their foreign boyfriends as "Only's" and regarded all of them as kept women in a very derogatory way. However, if some people talked behind our back, I thought they could talk as much as they wanted, but their talk did not hurt us.

Gus did not tell me much about Australia, and the only thing I knew about Australia was that a lot of sheep lived in the country. But when he said Australia was not so far from Bali, I remembered Shibayama who was killed in Ambon. I remember feeling closer to him and felt as if I could see him again by associating with somebody from Australia.

I did not tell my parents about Gus until I had a baby. How could I tell them that I was dating a foreign soldier? I am sure they were concerned when I went away often, but they also knew I was not the type of girl who would stay at home quietly. If a quiet girl started to do a similar thing as I did, they would of course be gravely worried, but I had already left home before. So maybe they were more or less resigned. Yet, they opposed it strongly when I said that I wanted to marry Gus. At the beginning, they talked as if I should be disowned as my association with the Australian soldiers would spoil marriage chances for my younger sisters and brothers. However, by the time I told of Gus, I had a baby. Also they realised I was getting too old to find a Japanese husband in an ordinary way in Japan. So I guess they eventually resigned themselves to the fact and accepted it.

Our baby was born in December 1948 and we named her Sumiko. We named her after our own names — Gus's "su" (in Japanese, Gus is

Michi (second from right) before she had Sumiko with her girlfriends in Kirikushi. All the women had Australian servicemen as boyfriends.

pronounced as "gasu") and Michi's "mi" and "ko" for a girl. Kirikushi was a good place to live because there were no MPs and there were other families like us. People in the area had been migrating to America for many years, so they had ties with America. So people were not hostile to us. At least, we did not feel any hostility. I heard a Japanese-American soldier came to visit his grandmother who lived in Kirikushi. Also the pay Gus brought back from the army was good and we could rent a big house for one pound a month because the exchange rate was very good for Australian currency.

You asked me why I wanted to have children when I knew I could neither marry an Australian soldier legally nor go to Australia with Gus. I had heard of so many cases where an Australian soldier left Japan for Australia and his girlfriend and child did not hear from him again. I heard of that more than enough. But when I look back, I wanted to have children as something to live for. I was already getting old and there was no prospect of marrying a Japanese man and having children with him. I did not have any other man whom I could think of marrying. Of course, there was no possibility of an arranged marriage for me. So I thought children would prop me up even though we would face difficulties. The fact that the children were mixed-race did not worry me much. There were many mixed-race children around, especially in Kure and Tokyo. We were told fathers of some were British and some others were American. I did not worry how those children would be treated in Japan because there were so many of them.

If Gus left us, I thought I could work and support myself and my children. I used to work for a newspaper company and had supported myself in Osaka and Tokyo. So I was confident that I could work. I was not really counting on Gus because I did not feel confident of his commitment. Looking back, it is rather puzzling, but I did not worry at all how I could manage with young children. When the worst came to worst, I knew I could resort to my family. In reality, they were so nice to us. They really treasured my children.

When I became pregnant with the second child, we seriously thought of having an abortion. Gus urged me to have an abortion. By the time we went to see a doctor, the pregnancy was too advanced for a routine abortion. I guess the doctor could have performed the operation if we had insisted, but he persuaded us against the idea. He was a religious Buddhist and said, "I can perform the abortion if you would die from the childbirth. But you are a healthy woman. You never know what will happen in the future. Let the baby be born." He was born in August 1950. At the end, this baby, George, became a very successful businessman and looks after me very well. So you really don't know, do you?

Gus was sent to Korea when the Korean War started. I went back to my mother's place in Tokushima with my children. My family welcomed us warmly. After two months, Gus came back and wrote to me to join him in Kirikushi again. Although I was happy then, I was constantly worried about him abandoning us. I heard so often that so-and-so was left behind by a soldier and ended up in tears. I did not think I wanted to be with him because I was attracted to his personality or to Australia. It was more a show of the feeling of people in the defeated nation to those of the victorious nation. I just did not want to worry about where the next food and clothes would be coming from. Gus as a young soldier wanted to enjoy himself and occasionally had casual affairs with other women. Sometimes he made it clear that he did not want to be tied down with a wife and children.

Finally, the transfer order arrived for Gus and he had to go back to Australia. Although Japanese wives were not allowed into Australia then, there was some prospect that permission would be given in the near future. Gus told me to wait until permission was given and he promised to apply to bring me and the children to Australia.

In December 1951, Gus left Japan for Australia. The night before his departure, he made love to me and promised to bring me and my children to Australia. But I was not sure whether he really meant it. All soldiers said the same thing, and I knew they did not always keep their word. I realised I had no choice but to go back to my mother's place and to look for work. On the day of departure, I went to see him off at the pier in Kure. I wrote my mother's address in Tokushima on a piece of paper and handed it to him. The children and I were going to stay there in the meantime. But I was not sure if he would keep the paper with him. He put the paper in his pocket, but if he decided to throw it away in the sea, then that would be the end of our ties. I was so sad to see him go that I cried out loud when I saw him off.

We went back to Tokushima to be with my family. They welcomed us warmly and treasured my children. But at night, I missed Gus and used to fall asleep in bed holding his pillow which still smelled of him. I thought I should go away to find a job in order to support myself and the children. I went to Osaka by myself to find a job, but I came back before long because I missed my children too much. One day, after a month and half, Gus's letter finally arrived. It said that he had started the process of bringing us to Australia and enclosed some money for us. I was so relieved to know that he had not abandoned us. The children did not need to grow up as fatherless kids. I could not help showing the letter to every visitor and telling them that he did not leave us behind after all. I told myself that, as a Japanese, I should make myself into a respectable housewife when I settled in Australia. Also I decided to be helpful to my parents-in-law even if various difficulties were presented to me. Gus regularly sent us 40,000 yen a month and that was more than enough for us to be comfortable.

The records at the National Archives of Australia showed that Gus submitted an application to bring Michi and the two children in March 1952. Thus, he did not seem to have had any hesitation to bring his Japanese family to Australia. In September of that year, he submitted English copies of the marriage certificate and birth certificates of the children. In a letter dated 19 January 1953, Gus was informed officially by the Ministry of Immigration that his application was successful and Michi and the children could be admitted to Australia.

Michi with four-year-old Sumiko and two-year-old George before their departure for Australia. This studio photograph was taken in Tokushima and sent to Gus in Australia.

I had heard of the White Australia policy, but I did not really know what it meant until I settled in Australia. At that time, I did not think Japanese would be discriminated against in Australia. I was happy to leave the hardships of the war and post-war time behind and go to a country where I believed there would be no hardship. When I look back I was thinking of going to a dream land where I would not need to worry about finding food. I did not learn English before our departure. I could think only of bringing my two children and myself to Australia to be with Gus, and packed our belongings and presents to the family in two tea chests. I was planning to study English after we arrived, but once I got there it was just not possible for me to do that anymore.

Chapter Three
Becoming an Australian Wife and Mother

THIS CHAPTER covers the period between Michi's migration to Australia and her settling down in this country. She arrived in Australia full of hope of establishing a new and happy life for herself and family. However, various difficulties awaited her as she needed to adapt to the new language and culture. Her narrative will reveal her struggle to realise stability and peace in her marriage and family.

Japanese immigrants in Australia before the arrival of war brides

Japanese migrated to Australia from the late nineteenth century mainly as contract labourers in the pearl and sugar cane industries in northern Australia. Wool buyers also arrived before the turn of the century and the first wool was exported by the Japanese buyers in 1890. At the beginning of this century, there were about 3,500 Japanese in Australia. After the Immigration Restriction Act was introduced in 1901, the number gradually decreased until the start of the Pacific War. The number of Japanese female migrants was never significant throughout the history of migration to Australia. In the early stages of Japanese migration, almost all of them were prostitutes. In 1897, the Commissioner of Police for Queensland reported that there were 116 Japanese women in the colony and that all but one, the consul's wife, were engaged in prostitution. Since the Immigration Restriction Act prohibited Japanese men from bringing their wives and fiancées to Australia, the number of Japanese women was always limited.[15]

30 At the start of the Pacific War in 1941, over 1,100 Japanese were in Australia, and were held in the internment camps as enemy aliens. Out of those, just over fifty were repatriated to Japan in 1942 as part of the prisoner exchange between Japan and Australia. The rest of them had to spend the war years in Australia with other Japanese internees who were sent from overseas, mainly from the Dutch East Indies. Later in the war, a number of Japanese POWs were also interned in various camps in Australia. After the war ended in the Japanese defeat, the decision was made by the Australian Government that all the Japanese nationals, resident or not, local or not, were to be repatriated. Exemption was given to just over 150 people including children, who were either Australian-born Japanese or married to an Australian or British-born spouse. Even the old pearl divers who had been living in Australia for over forty years were deported against their wishes to Japan, where they could no longer find any close relatives.[16] Consequently, when the Japanese women arrived in the 1950s, the Japanese population in Australia was negligible and the Japanese community non-existent.

From the first war brides' entry in 1952, the women were exempted from the notorious dictation test, but they were granted only five-year temporary visas: the government could deport them if it was thought necessary. They had to wait until 1956 for the government to change the requirements for citizenship applications so that they could obtain equal eligibility for citizenship with other immigrants. Most of the women became naturalised as soon as they were eligible, even though naturalisation meant the loss of their Japanese citizenship. There were several reasons for their swift action. Some women and their husbands were worried that the law could be reversed and their eligibility taken away. A lot of women believed that a wife should take up the nationality of her husband and children as a matter of course. Some women actually worried that, in the event of another war between Australia and Japan, Japanese citizens would be interned or deported just as in World War II. Some women whose husbands remained in the military services felt that, by retaining their Japanese nationality, they would hinder their husbands' career and promotion.

From the government's point of view, the assimilation process was completed when the women took up Australian citizenship. While the women were "dinkum Aussies" on paper, many women still had problems with the language and in adapting to the Australian way of life. However, those problems were buried in their busy family lives and the women turned to their husbands or more often to their children when they encountered language and other problems.

In the early 1950s when Japanese war brides arrived in Australia, the general sentiment towards Japan was not favourable. The memories of war were still vividly present in society as memoirs of Australian soldiers who were prisoners of war were published and war criminal trials were carried out.

Assimilation policy for immigrants

The war brides' arrival in the 1950s coincided with the entry of new immigrants to Australia mainly from the United Kingdom and other European countries. However, until the end of the war, Australia was predominantly Anglo-Celtic. According to the 1947 statistics, 89.7 per cent of the country's population was categorised as Anglo-Celtic, while Asians comprised only 0.8 per cent. The mass migration scheme, which was announced by Arthur Calwell, Minister for Immigration in the Chifley Labor government, was launched in 1945 in order to bring people to Australia with an unofficial slogan, "Populate or perish!" Between 1947 and 1952, there were 721,800 permanent arrivals, out of which 359,800 were British and 362,000 were non-British.[17] It was the non-British element, unprecedented in scale, that was transforming post-war Australia. By 1983, the total number of post-World War II immigrants had reached three million. However, it was ironic that Calwell, who was the enthusiastic advocate of immigration, remained the most fierce and persistent opponent of the admission of the Japanese wives.

Australia welcomed those new immigrants and expected them to be assimilated into existing Australian society as soon as possible. Australia's official attitude towards immigrants can be seen in the following statement made opposing the United Nations statement on minority rights. Here, Australia had "insisted that voluntary immigrant groups were intended to be assimilated into the community rather than be encouraged in an awareness of their different origin".[18]

A strong expectation of the government and the general public towards new immigrants was that they should and would adjust themselves to Australia and its predominantly British way of life. Harold Holt, who made the decision to admit Japanese war brides into Australia as Immigration Minister, stated at the 1952 Citizenship Convention that the government's intention in the immigration policy was to retain the British character as follows:

The British ... are a mixture of races. Australia, in accepting a balanced intake of other European people as well as British, can still build a truly British nation on this side of the world. I feel that if the central tradition of a nation is strong this tradition will impose itself on groups of immigrants, even if they are comparatively large.[19]

When the war brides walked up the gangplank in Kure to board the boats which would take them to Australia, they were determined to establish their new lives in their husbands' country. However, it was beyond anybody's anticipation, including their own, how difficult it would prove to be to become Australians. Michi's narrative in this chapter covers this in detail.

A boat leaving Kure for Australia in December 1953 with war brides on board as Australian servicemen and Japanese families bid them farewell. (Photo courtesy of Mrs S. Morris)

Michi's story

In March 1953, I left with Sumiko and George from Kure for Australia on a boat called the *Changte*. Sumiko was four years old and George was two. I packed our clothes and the presents for Gus's family into two tea chests to bring with us. Because the boat was leaving from Kure, the children and I travelled there with my mother and a brother and sister who wanted to see us off. Many villagers also gave me some money as a farewell present. It was nice to visit Kure again after a year and fond memories of when Gus was still in Japan came back to me vividly. The number of Australian soldiers did not seem to be as large as before, but they all walked with their Japanese girlfriends on their arms. I felt like calling out to those women and telling them that my Australian husband was taking us to Australia. I wanted to wish them the same luck as we had.

There were about twenty Japanese women on board the boat. Some of them were travelling with their husbands and some others were joining their husbands with their children like me. On the boat, just before the departure, the father of another war bride said to us, "As you are all going to a new country, I hope you will help and look after each other." He was getting emotional and almost choked with his words. His words still remain fresh in my memory.

When I was leaving Kure, I was not feeling sad at all. Actually, I just could not hide my joy and could not help smiling because I was so happy to join Gus in Australia. I also thought I was heading for a dream land and leaving all the hardship of the war behind. I thought I would not have to worry where tomorrow's food would come from once I arrived in Australia. In contrast, my mother was very sad to see us go. She cried aloud and shed so many tears that I thought her kimono sleeves were soaking wet. When I look back now, I understand how she must have felt then and feel sorry for her.

It took us almost a month to reach Australia. The boat stopped in Hong Kong for three or four days and we all went ashore. Although store vendors were trying to sell their goods to us by shouting, "Cheap! Cheap! Ten yen! Ten yen!" in Japanese, I could sense strong anti-Japanese feelings among the people there. Originally, we were going to travel on the previous boat, the *New Australia*, but I was told that there were going to be many single Australian soldiers on board the *New Australia* and those of us who were travelling without husbands were advised to travel on the *Changte*. On our boat there were about three other Japanese women who were accompanied by their husbands.

On the boat, I managed to get to know the other women and we exchanged our addresses in Australia. What we mainly talked about was where we were going to live in Australia. We managed to keep in touch for a while after our arrival, but I don't know how they are doing now. In contrast to the devastation which was still evident in Japan, the standard of fitting and furnishing in the boat was beyond my belief. I felt as if I was already in the dream land. The food on the boat was Western-style and I got bored with it quickly as the weather got stickier near the equator. All I could think of was the urge to have something which was not so greasy, such as pickled cucumber with *ochazuke* (a bowl of rice with green tea poured over it).[20] We discussed among ourselves what kind of food we would eat once we got off the boat. Some mentioned *sōmen* (cold noodle dipped in sauce) and others mentioned *kakigōri* (flaked ice with syrup). We never thought that such day-to-day Japanese dishes would be a rarity in Australia. I used to say that if I could eat pickled Chinese cabbage, I would be happy to die. A friend of mine heard about it and served it for me in Sydney many years later.

After stopping in Brisbane, the boat finally entered Sydney Harbour at night. I remember that the Harbour Bridge was lit up at night and it was very beautiful. I was excited, but at the same time I started to feel worried about the new life in Australia because I realised that I could not understand the language at all. Gus and his brother were there to meet us and I was so happy to see Gus after almost a year. I dressed myself in a green suit with a green hat for they were Gus's favourite. Sumi and George were overjoyed when they saw their father after many months. I was very glad to see their happy faces. I told myself that I should do whatever was necessary to hold on to this happiness. On our way to Gus's parents' house in Auburn, he taught me my first English sentence. It was "I laiki [like] Australia" and he told me to say it to everybody I would meet. This sentence was the first one and the last one that Gus ever taught me. He used to say that it was much easier for him to say things in Japanese than teaching me to speak English. When his mother came out to meet me and kissed me on the cheek, I repeated this sentence. I remember she was pleasantly surprised. Gus told me that she said, "I thought she did not speak a word of English, but she does." After I went into the house, I realised I could not understand what people were saying at all and I wondered how long it would take before I could adjust myself to the new life. It came to my mind that eating rice with pickled cucumber had to wait for a long time.

Gus is the ninth son in the family before a daughter was born finally after him. I saw a photo of young Gus when he was dressed more like a girl. After the arrival of the long-awaited girl, I guess he was not paid much attention. I found out that two of his elder brothers were killed in New Guinea during the war, fighting against the Japanese. His mother, however, did not mention a thing about them to me. His other brothers were also nice to me, but I had problems with one of their wives. She was quite hostile to me and ignored me completely for a long time, almost for twenty or thirty years. She worked as a nurse in New Guinea during the war and did not like Japanese at all. I remember she said, "It smells Japanese here" when she came into the kitchen when I was helping my mother-in-law. When Gus suggested to her that she talk to me, she said that she would not because I did not understand English at all. They eventually moved to Adelaide and we had more occasions to visit each other. However, she still refused to come into our house when I was present. She used to wait in the car while her husband was visiting us. When we visited their house, she did not talk to me at all. But she softened eventually and became nicer to me many years later. She started to ask after my health and even invited me to her parties. Of course, I did not bear a grudge against her when she wanted to be friendly, but it is not easy to forget how she had treated me initially.

Since I was admitted into Australia as a fiancée, Gus and I had our wedding ceremony at his mother's house on the fifth day after our arrival. I dressed myself in a kimono for the occasion. We already had two children and we had lived together for six years, so I felt as if I was remarrying somebody with my own children.

A week after the wedding, we left for Darwin where Gus was working at the Army base. I felt we were going on a honeymoon trip together. As we flew from Sydney to Darwin via Brisbane, we saw a wide spread of the land with pastures, sand, trees and jungles. When somebody told us that there were many crocodiles in those rivers, I realised we had come

Michi in kimono at her wedding in Sydney. She wore gloves at her mother-in-law's suggestion.

a long way away from Japan. It had been a bit chilly in Sydney, but in Darwin, it was very warm. Later, Gus used to complain that he had to pay for our travel from Sydney to Darwin when other war brides' travel expenses were covered by the government. After I arrived in Darwin, I was told that I was the first Japanese resident since the war. The destruction caused by Japanese bombing around the port was still evident. Although people were generally nice to me in the Army camp, I could sense a cold reception towards me as a Japanese in the town. When I went shopping, occasionally shopkeepers served other people first and kept me waiting even though the others came into the shop later than me. At that time, since I was unfamiliar with the country, I was not sure whether the shopkeepers saw me or not. But I could sense that something was going on.

Darwin was bombed 64 times by Japanese aircraft between February 1942 and November 1943. The first two attacks which took place on 19 February caused the biggest damage with 243 casualties and between 300 and 400 injuries. In these air raids, twenty military aircraft were destroyed, eight ships at anchor in the harbour were sunk, and most civil and military facilities in Darwin were destroyed. As Darwin residents and military personnel believed that the Japanese invasion was imminent, a large-scale exodus to the south occurred afterwards. Approximately half Darwin's civilian population ultimately fled and this incident later became known as "The Adelaide River Stakes".

One day, a man stopped me in the town and asked me if I was from Japan. When I answered yes to his question he introduced himself. He was a Japanese Australian and kept his father's Japanese family name, Hasegawa, during the war in spite of the hostility towards the Japanese. He asked me why I came to Australia. I did not know why he asked the question then, but later I realised he actually wanted to ask me why I had chosen to come to Australia where discrimination against the Japanese was still very strong. I never saw him again. On another occasion, an old Chinese man in a fish shop started to speak to me in Japanese. He said, "There used to be many Japanese in Darwin and they were all nice people. They all went back to Japan after the war. I used to know a lady whose name was Yoshiko. I cannot forget about her and am still waiting for her return." He told me that he wanted to talk about many things with me and asked me to return with a deep bow. I was expecting my third child then and went back to the shop some weeks after the birth of the baby. He was not there any more and I was told he died only four days before. I regretted that I could not have visited him earlier.

Several months after our arrival, a colleague of my husband brought two Japanese men to our house. A Japanese fishing boat came into Darwin for the first time after the war and its crew wanted to visit me when they heard there was only one Japanese woman living in Darwin. I was so overwhelmed to see Japanese faces and hear Japanese that I started to cry in front of them. They invited Gus and me to their boat and served us *sukiyaki*. Gus was happy to drink sake and I was so happy to see two slices of pickled radish on a plate.

Gus started to drink soon after we settled in Darwin. After work, he went straight to the canteen and did not come home till one or two in the morning. I used to stay up and wait for his return at night. One difficult custom I had to get used to in the camp was to attend parties in the evenings with my husband. That was the hardest thing I had to do because I hated to leave my children on their own at night without anybody to watch them. Sumiko was only four and George was two. We had to put them in bed and lock the bedroom door before we left.

I heard many couples did the same. I was so worried about my children and felt awful thinking of them crying in the dark. Yet, I had no choice. Gus kept drinking and drinking and did not come home unless I attended those parties with him. I did not enjoy being at parties because I could not speak English and I did not drink or smoke. Gus used to move to his friends' table to drink and I was left alone by myself all through the evenings.

I had a funny experience around that time. One night, Gus brought his friend home after a drinking session. In Japan, when a husband brings his guests home, his wife should entertain them well. Therefore, I served them food and other things in order to entertain them. Then, Gus started to bring his friends back to our house more frequently and I had to do a lot of work for them late at night. It was also getting expensive to serve them with food and drinks. I started to feel desperate, but I still thought a good wife should look after her husband's friends well. Finally, I asked him why his friends started to visit us more often. Gus was surprised to hear me ask this question, and said he did that because I enjoyed looking after them. I was doing all that work just to please Gus, not for myself!

Sumiko started preschool in Darwin soon after we arrived and started to learn English very quickly. Although I was planning to study English after I arrived in Australia, I did not have a chance to do that at all. I became pregnant with my third child in Darwin and was busy looking after two small children. Gus used to tell me to learn English, but what could I do? He did not teach me any and did not find a teacher for me. I did not have money for lessons and time to study. I could say "Hello" and "Good morning" to our neighbours, but my English was not good enough to hold any meaningful conversations with them. In our household, Gus and I were speaking in Japanese and I used to talk to my children in Japanese with some English words. The children always answered in English. They never wanted to speak Japanese. I did not know how it worked, but my children could understand what I was saying. For example, when I said to them "bring a broom" in Japanese, they did bring a broom. When the children were a bit older, they sometimes complained that they could not understand what I was saying, especially when I was scolding them. According to them, I used to get upset further when I heard their complaints and told them to go to a Japanese school to learn Japanese. I do not remember saying that, but that was what Sumiko said to me. The funny thing is that Sumiko is now attending a Japanese language course at night. Finally, she is in a Japanese school.

Initially I wanted to go to church in Australia because I had attended church for six months in Japan before I came. At that time, I needed to have a reference from a minister to obtain a permit to come to this country. The minister had suggested to me that I should be baptised once I settled in Australia. I attended a few church services in Australia but I did not know what they were saying. So I stopped going. The problems with the language occurred when I went shopping soon after we arrived in Australia. I could not understand the price of goods so I used to pay in notes and receive change in coins. We used to end up with a big pile of coins at home!

Payment of £16 every fortnight was made to me by the Army as an allotment. The money Gus had sent us in Japan was more than sufficient there, but in Australia it was hard to make ends meet with that amount. The amount was directly paid from the Army to me and I did not know how much Gus actually earned. Gus kept the rest of his salary for himself and spent it for his pleasure. I never thought of asking him how much he had been paid, or of asking him to increase the amount of my allotment. I somehow believed that I needed to manage within the amount I received. Actually, the payment from the Army did not increase at all although the number of the children increased steadily. So child endowment from the government was the only other source of income for me. Although the amount from the government increased according to the number of children, it was not easy to manage the growing household.

Our time in Darwin was a very difficult one for me. By the time I had the third child, Wayne, I had to make up my mind to settle down in Australia. I realised that there was no option for me to go back to Japan. But I often thought later that I would have walked back to Japan with my children if I could. Since there was an ocean between Australia and Japan, I could never do that. Around this time, I remember Shibayama often appeared in my dreams at night. In those dreams, he just stared at me with a concerned look without saying anything. I felt he still cared about me. I used to think about him often when I was faced with hardship and sadness. Then I told myself that I should persevere in the hardship so that I should be able to secure happiness at the end.

After eighteen months in Darwin, Gus was transferred to Wallangarra in northern New South Wales. We moved often because of Gus's work. In fact, we moved eight times in eleven years! I guess he must have asked for transfers for himself. He never asked me if I wanted to move or stay. At the same time, I did not object to his decision. Basically, I did not mind moving because I liked to see new places and the Army moved our furniture for us. But packing and unpacking were a lot of work. Often, we found the sizes of windows were different in each house and it was awkward to hang ill-fitting curtains on them. When we arrived in a new place, Gus went to the camp for drinks to see his mates straight away, and I was left to do the unpacking on my own. I wished Gus would help me, but I almost gave up on him. At the same time, I was worried he might leave us if I made too much fuss. I knew a few cases in the camps when husbands left their wives and the women had to fend for themselves. I would not have known what to do on my own with small children in a country where I did not know the language. I had no idea where and how I could support my children and myself. Yet, probably, it would have been better if I had stood firm and expressed my opinions to him then. With the transfers, the children needed to change their schools often and that was hard for them. I do not know how many schools Sumiko went to. I think she went to several different primary schools and high schools.

Michi and baby Frances outside their house in Wallangarra in 1956.

After leaving Darwin, we went to Sydney to stay with Gus's mother until a house was ready for us in Wallangarra. She was not very welcoming at the beginning and did not seem to be pleased to see a new grandson, Wayne. Although she herself had ten children, she never approved of me having many children. She often spoke as if it was my own fault for having so many children, and not her son's. After spending about a week with her, we moved to Wallangarra on an overnight train from Sydney. There I met a Japanese woman, Fumiko, who had also married an Australian soldier and we became firm friends for many years to come. There were some other Japanese women in the camp, who had married Australian soldiers. We went shopping together and talked in Japanese among ourselves at parties. I had not realised how much it meant for me to have friends who spoke the same language. I felt I could laugh from the bottom of my heart only when I spoke Japanese.

We spent two years in Wallangarra. It was a quiet place with pasture all around the camp and I had my fourth and fifth children, Frances and Robert, there. After that period, we moved to Bogan Gate near Parkes. When I was in Bogan Gate, I wrote an essay and sent it in for an essay contest run by a Japanese women's monthly magazine, *Shufu no tomo*.[21] I won the contest and the essay was published in Japan under the title "The Rough Road a War Bride Had to Take".

Michi did not have a copy of the essay with her when I interviewed her in Adelaide. However, she told me the title and approximate year of publication, and this enabled me to locate it in the Shufu no tomo Archive in Tokyo. The essay was published in 1958 and Michi's account during the interviews accurately matched the essay which was written over forty years ago. The following section is mainly based on an excerpt from the essay.

> After we settled in the Wallangarra Camp, Gus started to stay away from home till late on many evenings. He always had some excuses, such as attending meetings, playing card games, or listening to his friends' woes. I tried to believe him but I could not deny his attitudes towards the family had changed. He was not caring for the children and shouted at me for trivial things.
>
> On a pay day, two weeks before Christmas, he did not come home for lunch or dinner and at midnight he was still not home. Cars approached from the distance, but all of them passed our

house and drove away, just lighting the windows. I was distressed and started to cry. When I looked outside through the window, I could see a house with bright lights on and I was just gazing at it with my teary eyes. The house belonged to a woman whose husband was away on duty. She had a bad reputation in the camp. The lights went off and on and I wondered what she was doing in the middle of the night. Then a man left the house, was seen off by a woman, and got into a car. The car arrived at our house with Gus.

Shocked to realise what was happening, I shouted at him. Gus tried to tell me that I saw the wrong person, but I was not convinced. Finally, I asked him if I could do anything to change the situation. Then he said, "You don't know anything about Australia and you do not understand English." He probably wanted to say that was why he felt lonely. I was really hurt by his words and shouted, "You knew that already when you married me, and you said that was fine. You do not even try to teach me anything. You are a bad husband."

The next day, I went to the woman's house with all of his clothes from the previous night. When she answered the door in her nightgown and realised I was there, she was surprised and asked if I wanted to come in. I refused to go in, but demanded that she clean the clothes and return them to me. Gus was so surprised with my strong reaction that he apologised and asked for forgiveness. Thereafter, I tried to do my best to keep his attention from anything other than home and myself. You might think it was ridiculous, but I would not let him go out at night. I used to go to pick him up from the parties when he was late. I was desperate to keep him.

I also repented myself. I realised that I had neglected Gus because of the children. I also did not look after myself enough to be attractive to him. I used to blame him for various problems. So I tried to do things differently. It took almost a year before our relationship was mended, but eventually we went back to our normal selves and the children were also happy to be in a peaceful atmosphere.

Michi and Gus with their five children and Gus's mother in 1957. This photo accompanied her Japanese essay which won a prize in 1958.

After two years in Wallangarra, we moved to Bogan Gate, another country town near Parkes. Our house was away from the camp and stood by itself in the woods. I hardly saw anybody other than my children. I had five children by then. Sumiko was eight years old. She helped me around the house and looked after her younger brothers and sister after she came home from school. On weekends, she prepared breakfast for me and brought it to my bed because she said, "Saturday and Sunday are Mummy's holidays." She was the top student in her class even though I could not help her with her schoolwork at all. The children learned Australian history at school and taught me about it at home. I occasionally heard that they had a hard time because they were part-Japanese. In those instances, I said to them, "You are proper Australians. Study hard and do better than those who bully you."

Probably, I was expecting too much from Gus. In spite of my efforts, Gus did not seem happy and started gambling on horse races. I tried my best to cheer him up, and tried not to complain about his gambling. I put on a cheerful face even when he came home late. But one weekend he did not return home. He made an excuse and said that he was playing poker games till late. I could not trust his words at all and accused him of not caring for his family properly. He listened to my woes silently and said, "I won't be happy if you are not happy."

I knew he had some worries. I heard that he had a fight with somebody who said that all the Japanese women who came to Australia were ex-prostitutes. I also heard that those servicemen who had married Japanese women would experience difficulties getting promotions at work. I was the only Japanese in Bogan Gate and I could sense some people were looking at me with unfavourable perspective. I thought our marriage was near to breaking up and wanted to go back to Japan. When I asked my children if they wanted to go back to Japan with me, Sumiko said, "I would go for a visit, but not to stay there for good." However, Gus told me he wanted to apply to go to Malaya by himself for two years and suggested I should wait for him in Japan with the children. Since I did not know what to do, I finally decided to go to see Fumiko, who was still in Wallangarra.

I took the two younger children with me to Wallangarra and left the older ones with Gus. It was nice to see Fumiko after many months. I talked about the problems we had at home. In contrast to our home, Fumiko's home seemed to be surrounded by warmth and I wondered what went wrong for Gus and me. However, soon after we arrived there, I received an urgent telegram which read that Gus had left for Darwin and I should get back as soon as possible as the children were being looked after by our neighbour. I could not understand what was going on. Did Gus decide to leave for Malaya from Darwin after all? Did he leave us behind? I had to rush to catch the next available train to get back to my children.

When I arrived back in Bogan Gate after two days' travel from Wallangarra, the children were very happy to see me and started to tell me what happened while I was away. Sumiko said she was the first in a running race and won a toy as a prize. Then the next thing she said devastated me. She said a man and a woman came to visit while I was away. The man went home, but the woman stayed behind and Gus drove her home the next morning. Then, Wayne complained that his father did not play with him much because there was a lady visiting the house. When I heard it I had to go out of the house because I could not control myself in front of my children.

Michi told me in detail what the children said about the woman when I interviewed her. When Sumi said, "The lady spent her time on Mummy's bed and she had a nightie with her in a bag," Michi burst into tears in front of the children. Realising the distress those words caused her mother, Sumiko quickly stopped her brothers reporting further.

In spite of those heartbreaking experiences, I decided to remain in Australia and bring up our children as Australians. I just hoped that Gus would eventually realise his responsibilities as a father. They do not have anybody else as their father other than Gus. After spending two months in Darwin, Gus came back and behaved as if nothing had happened between us. I did not object to that because I also wanted to have a fresh start.

(End of excepts from the *Shufu no tomo* magazine article)

I was happy to win the essay contest. Not only was the essay published, but I was also awarded some prizes. The editor wrote to me to say that they would send me some Japanese goods instead of money because it was not easy to transfer money to Australia. I remember receiving Japanese foods, such as *miso* paste, in Bogan Gate. It was such a treat for me. However, some time later, I found out that my mother had read the essay in Japan. She was so distressed to learn that I had a hard time in Australia with my husband, that she could not sleep at night with worry for almost two months! I regretted that I had written that essay and felt sorry for my mother. After that I never wrote an essay nor a letter with anything bad or worrying to my family in Japan.

When we were living in Bogan Gate, one day Sumiko came home and asked me if her father was stupid. I wondered why she asked me such a question. She said somebody at school said to her that her father must have been stupid to marry a Japanese woman when there were many women in Australia. Of course, I answered "no" to her question, but I assumed the children must have heard those comments occasionally outside home. However, they did not talk much about those incidents with me.

The next camp we moved to was Moorebank near Sydney in 1960 and I had my seventh and last child there. It was nice to live in an Army camp with other families again. When I heard that there was another Japanese wife in the camp, I wanted to see her desperately. At the same time, I was worried whether I could speak Japanese properly. While I was in Bogan Gate, I did not have anybody to speak Japanese with for three years. When I finally saw the lady, I felt as if I saw my own sister after many years of separation and could not stop crying.

There, I met a Scottish woman called Betty, who had married an Englishman. She persuaded me to go out and mix with people. Until then, I did not have much chance to meet people because I had so many children to look after. My English did not improve much and I could exchange greetings in English, but not much more. Betty said, "Michi, you should not stay only at your house. You can rely on Sumiko to look after the younger ones. You need to spend an hour or two outside your home." She suggested I should learn to play darts with her. While we were playing together at the canteen, she taught me English. She talked to me in English and I wanted to understand her and respond to her. That was how I learned English. After those "lessons", I finally managed to have enough confidence to carry out conversations in English. So, it took me almost ten years before I could have conversations in English.

Sumiko told me that she used to accompany her mother as an interpreter from a young age and had responsibility for looking after her brothers and sister while her parents were out. Michi said she brought Sumiko along to the hospital when the younger ones had measles and chicken pox. Sumiko understood Michi and interpreted her words to the doctors. When I asked Sumiko how she felt doing those tasks for her mother, she answered, "It was not so difficult, but it surely made me grow up faster."

I applied for Australian citizenship and was naturalised in 1962 while we were in Moorebank. Gus said that I should become an Australian citizen and arranged everything for me. I did not need to prepare for a test as war brides in the United States had to do. I could not have done that then because I did not understand much English. At the ceremony, as everybody else was handing his or her passport in before receiving a new Australian passport, I handed my Japanese passport in as well. Later, a few friends of mine showed me their Japanese passports even though they

Michi in 1964, dressed up for an Army party.

had Australian citizenship. When I asked them why they kept their passports, they said, "Since nobody told us to return our Japanese passports, we kept them."

At one of those parties in the camp, I wore a Japanese shawl over my dress. While many people admired it and made nice comments, a woman in her fifties approached me and pulled the shawl off my shoulders. After rolling it up, she threw it on the ground and stepped on it. She shouted me and said, "Go back to Japan." She was obviously drunk. Gus watched the incident but did not intervene or say a word. He might have been suffering from the inferiority complex of having a Japanese wife.

In 1963, we moved to the Broadmeadows Camp in Melbourne. It was getting more and more difficult to manage a household with seven children with the limited amount of income. The allotment from the Army did not seem to increase even though I had seven children by then. The children's endowment did increase, but it did not cover the cost of bringing up growing children and educating them. One day, our neighbour suggested that I should go out to work. She said, "Michi, why don't you go out to work. It must be difficult to manage with so many children. I will look after your younger kids." She offered to mind my youngest son, who was about preschool age, for five dollars a week during the day.

A Japanese friend who was working in a telephone factory suggested that I apply there because they needed people who were clever with their hands. The language was not a problem at all because we did not have to talk much. It was more a matter of skilfulness of the fingers. They showed me where the wires needed to be connected and I soldered them at the appropriate sections. So I started to work in the wiring section between seven and four every day. I really enjoyed working there. I never realised how much fun it was to work because I could get out of the house and mix with people. My supervisor was very happy to have me because I could finish five items while others were struggling to finish three. I worked there for about a year and a half until we moved to Adelaide because of Gus's transfer. Before leaving for work, I set breakfast on the table in the morning and prepared dinner for the family after coming home in the afternoon. Gus was not involved in the family life at all. Although my older children helped me around the house, such as collecting firewood for the hot water, I was too busy to remember how I brought my children up. To tell the truth, I do not remember about Frances when she was young at all. Why don't you ask her how I brought her and the other children up when you see her? Sumiko told me I used to place rows of bread slices on the table to butter them and make many sandwiches, but I do not remember that either.

While we lived in Melbourne I joined the Sōka Gakkai.[22] I had so many problems with Gus, but I could not ask for help from my parents who were so far away. I felt other Japanese women avoided me when I was in Melbourne. Maybe because I had too many children, we started to have a reputation that our children were unruly. A Japanese wife told other women that my house was always messy. But with five sons, how could we keep them under control all the time? Also they might have worried that I would visit them with all my children if they invited me. One day, Miyuki, another war bride in Melbourne, asked me if I was interested in attending a Sōka Gakkai meeting. She did not know much about the religion, but was curious because the religion came from Japan and chanted some Buddhist chants which had been familiar to me. At the first meeting, I was impressed to see an Australian man chant seriously while he sat on the floor with folded legs. Also I felt people who gathered there seemed pleasant. Those things really moved me and I decided to join the sect straight away and came home with a sacred scroll, a string of prayer beads and a scripture book. I could understand what they were teaching as well. Basically, they were teaching that we were the ones who needed to solve problems, but the religion can give us some help. Even though I had to leave Melbourne soon after I joined, I have been a member of the sect ever since.

After Melbourne, we moved to Adelaide in 1965. All of us travelled together for the first time on the train. When we arrived at Adelaide railway station, I remember a waitress's astonished look when Gus and I and our seven children were having breakfast at a station restaurant. Sumiko had graduated from high school in Melbourne and started a job at the Commonwealth Bank there, but she asked for a transfer to Adelaide. She actually wanted to become a teacher, but gave that up in order to help me and her younger brothers and sister financially. George was studying at a technical school in Melbourne, but he was also transferred to another technical school in Adelaide. I did not want to move any more because of the children's education and work.

Although neither Gus nor myself were attentive enough toward our children's education, most of them did very well at school. I did not have any spare time to worry about their schooling because I was busy working. Gus was not interested in the children at all. If a school teacher wanted to talk to us about a child, neither of us wanted to see the teacher. Gus did not want to be involved with family matters and I could not understand English very well. Actually, I did not know our third son, Robert, won a Commonwealth scholarship with the top score among 500 students, until a Japanese friend whose husband worked for a newspaper congratulated me. In spite of winning the scholarship, he did not want to continue his schooling so that he could go to university. I was worried that he was missing a great chance, but Gus was not interested in his son's decision, so I consulted George, our eldest son. George said that it was up to Robert whether he wanted to go to university or not. If he did not want to go, George said, nobody could force him to go. I was not convinced, but maybe that is the way people think in Australia. What he did instead was to leave home with his friends without telling us the destination. Later, I learned that they went fruit-picking. Parents of his friends thought Robert was the leader and came to see us to find out where they had gone. We did not know either. I felt worried and embarrassed at the same time. Robert's friends came home before long because they found fruit-picking was too much hard work. But Robert did not come home for a while because he thought it was such fun.

Chapter Four
Later Years

MICHI CONTINUES her narrative in this chapter and talks about her life in more recent years, between 1970 and the present. As the children grew up and became more independent, Michi started to explore other activities outside home. But marriage stability for which she had been striving the whole time she was in Australia did not come easily for her. She also looks back on her life course and reflects upon her experience as a war bride.

Michi's story

In 1969, Gus retired as a Sergeant Major in the Army after 26 years and we finally settled down in Adelaide. Since we all liked the sea, we bought a house near the beach. I was working as a housemaid at a hotel between seven o'clock in the morning till four in the afternoon. I worked hard at the hotel. Although my job was mainly to tidy up the bedrooms, I helped in the kitchen when I finished with the upstairs rooms and did waitressing for the breakfast. Since I was willing to help out with any type of work, they appreciated me very much. I did not want people to think Japanese were lazy. I knew the Japanese had a reputation as hard-working people and I wanted to live up to that reputation. Many of my colleagues at the hotel were Italian women and we all got along very well. Actually, we still keep in touch. The manager liked me a lot and he still calls out to me when he sees me on the street. Since his voice is loud when he calls out, it is rather embarrassing. But it is nice of him to remember me so fondly years after my service in the hotel.

At Sumiko's wedding. George and young Ronald are on the far left, Frances is second adult from the right.

In 1969, my eldest child, Sumiko, got married. I was very happy on the wedding day and I wrote the following in Japanese on the back of her wedding photograph:

> My dearest daughter,
> I would never have got through all the difficulties without you. You have been my inner strength. You comforted me when we were sad. We have been joyful together in the happy times. You are everything to me. On this fine Easter Saturday in 1969, the clear blue sky is here to bless you. I say thank you and all your friends at your wedding. When I touched your wedding dress my tear drops made a small mark on the dress … At the church I could not understand all the words [the] minister spoke, but I listened to them very intently. After the ceremony Sumiko and Kerry waved and headed for the hotel. I will be so lonely without you. I miss you so much around the house. I kept telling myself that you were not far away from me, so I should not be so lonely. Happiness is not something you are born with but must build up by yourself. Do build up your happiness with Kerry.
> From your Mother[23]

Unfortunately, Sumiko later divorced her husband, but now she has remarried.

In 1970, I finally made my first trip back to Japan. Almost a year before the trip, I wrote to my mother, who was living with my brother at the time, that I was going to come back and both of us were really looking forward to seeing each other. Gus gave me the money for tickets and I provided my own pocket money. Although I could not afford to bring much money back to Japan, it was not a big problem because the exchange rate for the Australian dollar was very good at around 450 yen. A hundred dollars could buy quite a lot in Japan then.[24] That was the very first time I went away without my children. I remember that my youngest son who was nine years old cried at the airport, saying he wanted to go with me. It was such a joy to be back in Japan after seventeen years, although a lot of things had changed during my absence. The streets looked different with many new houses. The station names had been changed and it was difficult to find my friends' houses. I realised that my mother had gone to the station to meet me five hours before the train was due to arrive. Furthermore, she kept my wedding photo by her bed. She must have been missing the child who had gone furthest away.

I stayed in Japan for three weeks. Although I was very happy to be back in Japan, I missed my children terribly. I kept wondering if they were eating properly or doing well. My mother sensed my feeling and pointed this out to me by saying, "You had better go back to Australia soon. Your heart has already flown back to Adelaide." She used to save up her pension money and occasional income from sewing in order to give it to me when I went home. The amount was around 100,000 yen and I guess she gave me almost all the amount she had saved. She was living peacefully with my brother's family. It was nice to see her contented. Witnessing her happiness in her old age, I hoped I would be able to achieve a similar outcome for myself eventually. Compared with the troubles she had experienced, my problems with Gus looked minute. I thought I should be able to handle and manage them well.

I managed to make a second trip to Japan in 1974 with Sumiko, her two young children and Frances. At that time, a local newspaper reporter came to interview us and an article was published in the paper. He wrote as if that was the very first time that I had gone back, but actually

Michi's family welcomes her on her arrival in Tokushima in 1970 after seventeen years in Australia. First on the left is Michi's mother and the third from the left is Michi.

Visiting Michi's mother in Tokushima in 1974 with Sumiko (middle on right), Frances (next to Sumiko) and Sumiko's two sons (front right).
(Michi is not in this photo.)

it was the second time for me and the first time for my children. I said in the article, a lot of things had changed in Japan during my absence. The economic development made Japan a much more affluent country than in the 1950s. When I left Japan in 1953, people did not have much, but, in twenty years or so, the situation was all different. Of course, inflation had been tremendous, and things were all incredibly expensive. I felt as if I had just woken up from a long sleep and had trouble catching up with changes. My mother was very happy to see her granddaughters and great grandchildren. I remembered that she kept calling Sumiko's two sons Sumiko and George. I guess they reminded her of Sumiko and George when they had stayed with her in Tokushima before we left for Australia.

In the article, the subheading said "Living a comfortable life as an Australian citizen". Although she talked about some hostility towards Japan in Darwin in the 1950s, it is not possible to detect the hard life Michi had to endure from the article at all. It said that the family lived happily in a quiet academic city, Adelaide.

Later, I went back to Japan with George and his family. George was very much impressed with the economic growth in the country where he had been born. Being half-Japanese used to be something he could not boast about, but he said that he now felt proud to have Japanese blood. I think he decided to start his own business then, and he runs a very successful business in Western Australia now. He told me his friends thought one of the reasons for his success was the work ethic which came from his Japanese background. As he was only two when we left Japan, he did not go to school in Japan at all. I do not think I had ever formally taught my children a Japanese way of working or thinking. Probably, he just watched me while he was growing up.

Gus was working for an accounting firm after he retired from the Army. Since his lifestyle had changed drastically, his health suffered and he lost a lot of weight, but he eventually got used to civilian life. He and I did not have any big problems around that time. I was still at the hotel working from seven to four. The children were growing up. In 1979, Gus and I had a holiday together in Europe. On the way there, we stopped in Japan for him to meet my family for the very first time. He never had a chance to meet my family while he was in Japan during the occupation.

I left my job at the hotel before I turned sixty-one (in 1980). I started to experience back problems and I was worried I might become stooped just like my mother did. Since I had worked hard for years, I did not mind staying at home. There were still many things to do at home. Meals needed to be cooked and the house needed to be cleaned. I prepared nice breakfasts for my family.

Then a very sad thing happened in February 1981. My youngest son committed suicide. I did not sense anything before he killed himself. When I look back, I could remember he seemed rather subdued around that time, but we could not foresee anything.[25] After our youngest son's death, Gus suffered a lot and became depressed. Similarly, it took a very long time for me to come to terms with my son's death. One thing I pledged was to grow flowers in my garden so that I could bring them to his grave. In 1982, I decided to visit the head temple of Sōka Gakkai in Japan with other followers from Australia in order to pray for my son's spirit. That was the first time I visited the head temple even though I had joined the sect almost twenty years ago. I was impressed during this visit by the eagerness and sincerity many followers expressed at the head temple which was located near Mt Fuji. I could renew my belief and felt more positive about my future.

I did not join the Sōka Gakkai in order to meet other Japanese. That was not my intention. In Adelaide, there are currently very few Japanese members in our sect and the majority of them are either Australians or people from other countries. I am the only war bride among our local members. Other war brides in this city are generally happy, without many problems. Their husbands are nice and they did not experience much misfortune. I do not think they needed religion at all. I believe there are about ten war brides who are Sōka Gakkai members in Melbourne. At our meetings, although we chant in Japanese, all the discussion and teaching are in English. Other members wonder if I can follow the English discussions. Although the details of the discussion are not clear to me, I can understand what has been discussed more or less instinctively as I have trained for all those years in Australia. Also, I treasure the interactions of different types of people at the meetings. That is why I can happily sit in the discussion even though I usually do not speak up.

When Michi was the South Australian state representative of Sōka Gakkai in the early 1990s, Tina Turner, a rock singer, held a concert in Adelaide. As a devout follower of the religion, Ms Turner wanted to meet other members and pray together, so she contacted Michi and decided to come to see her to chant the prayer. Michi did not know how famous Tina Turner was. When she arrived with her bodyguards and entourage Michi realised Ms Turner was somebody famous, but she was not impressed with her "funny hair-do" and mini-skirt which did not suit her age. By the time the chanting session was finished, the neighbours realised who was visiting Michi's small flat and a crowd gathered outside her residence.

At home, everything was peaceful after my son's death. The other children were growing up and becoming more independent. I was at home and had more time to myself than before. I thought it was such happiness for a wife to wait for her husband's return and enjoy having meals and chats with him at home. On a typical day, we watched TV after dinner and went to bed at 10:30. On weekends, we went out together. After the earlier difficult years, I thought I could finally enjoy an ordinary happiness at home. Such peaceful days lasted for eight years. I thought I had finally obtained the ultimate happiness as a woman after a long struggle.

One day, when I went shopping, a shop assistant in a dress shop asked me how long I had been in Australia. I answered, "I have been in Australia for thirty-three years. I have eleven grandchildren and seven children. I lost one son, but the rest are all independent and happy." Then, the assistant said, "Wonderful! You have contributed so much to Australia. It must have been difficult for you, but I really appreciate your contribution in bringing up those who support the country." For me, her words sounded as if they came from god. On the other hand, some people were still ignorant. At a party, my husband and I were talking to another couple who seemed to have had a lot of drink. The wife asked me where I was from, so I answered Japan. Then she asked me which part of China Japan was. Then we started to talk about children. When she heard that I had seven children, she commented with laughter, "Our dog just gave birth to seven puppies last week as well. It is the same as you, isn't it?" I realised that there was such a difference in people's perceptions. The former sounded glorious, the latter sounded as if they were words from demons.

I felt so contented that I told myself to work hard in order to retain those peaceful days at home. But this happiness did not last for long. Gus retired from the company job in 1986 and started to work as manager at a local yacht club. The work started at four in the afternoon and he did not come home till very late at night. I was worried about the job because he needed to work in the club, serving drinks to customers. I was not sure whether he could stay away from alcoholic drinks when he had to serve them. In addition, they said many people who previously worked in that position experienced marriage problems and divorce. Yet, Gus was so pleased to find a job locally that I could not stop him. For about six months he worked there without any incidents, so I thought I was worried over nothing. I had already planned to visit Japan again with other Sōka Gakkai followers. About a week before our departure, Gus said he wanted to come along with me. However, I told him that it was impossible to arrange for another person to go at such short notice and left on my own. I should have brought him with me because I was going to be away for six weeks instead of a few weeks as usual. By the time I came back to Adelaide I could sense something was going on.

When I was away, my second son, Wayne, and the two younger sons were living at home with Gus. That was the reason I had been able to go away for a longer period than usual. The boys said they would look after their father. Wayne had come back to Adelaide from Perth after his divorce and he was keen to meet another lady. Apparently, he went out every night and told his father how much fun he had. I guessed such talk awakened Gus's habit which had been dormant for a while. By the time I came back, Gus was drinking a lot and seeing another woman as if he wanted to catch up what he had missed in the previous years. I blamed myself that I had left him behind, and tried to change his mind. I had to repeat all the things I used to do many years ago all over again, such as staying up late to wait for Gus to return. But this time he did not want to come back. He said that he did not want to be tied down by his family and wanted a life of his own. I asked him what he would do if he got sick when he did not have anybody who could look after him. His answer was that he would just go to hospital. He said, "I do not want to be tied down by my family any more. I do not like my children and grandchildren anyway. I want to be on my own and do what I want to do for the rest of my life. I do not want to be bothered by anybody and I want to be free." He even told me to go back to Japan and marry a Japanese man. A woman who was reaching seventy years? Remarry? Go back to Japan?

Finally, I made up my mind. One day when he was not around, I packed my belongings and left. I always thought perseverance was the most important virtue for a Japanese woman. My mother persevered through all the misdeeds of my father for all those years. In her old age, she was finally rewarded by obtaining peace. I told myself I should do the same since my mother had done that, and tolerate my husband's misbehaviour. However, I realised I had already changed into an Australian woman. I could not take Gus's selfish acts any more and had to leave him. My children all supported my decision. In a way, they urged me to leave. Sumiko said she did not want to see me cry any more. Sumiko and George said that they would look after me. Other children said, "It is better for you to be without him." Frances rented a vacant house next to her for me and I moved in there. Soon after I moved out, the two younger sons decided to move in with me because they did not want to live with their father.

Although I made the decision to leave, I was devastated. I cried and cried and hated Gus fiercely. In many ways, I did not want to leave him. Although I had known that Gus was not a respectable man, I left Japan for that man and persevered through all the hardships for forty years. It was not as easy to sever such a tie with him as the children had expected. My children did not mind leaving their partners when things did not work out. When Frances had a divorce, she said that it was not difficult to leave the situation she was in and that it was easy to start again. However, I could not think that way so easily. I had made a commitment to Gus forty years ago and persevered though all the hardship. If the marriage ended up in divorce, all the hardship I endured would have resulted in nothing.

I was so upset that I tore up all the photos of Gus. I did that with even our wedding pictures, so I only have photos of me at the wedding now, not of him. Since I lost a lot of weight after the separation, my family in Japan was very surprised to see me so thin when I went back soon after the separation. When I was asked what was the matter, I could not tell them I had left him because of the problems with women and drinking. If I told them what actually happened between Gus and I, my family would have been very worried, especially my mother. She would be very sad and upset for me because she remembered how she had felt when my father acted in a similar way as Gus. I did not want her to stir up the agony again. So I told them that I was distressed because Gus had died.

60   Of course, they expressed their sympathy, and they gave me condolence money, which I was not expecting.[26] I had completely forgotten that gifts of condolence money were customary in Japan when somebody close died. Although I was surprised, I could not change my story then. Then, my mother wrote to me later to tell me that she had arranged return gifts for the money I received. Again, I had completely forgotten that I needed to make return gifts by using a certain proportion of the money. Since my mother organised all that and also paid for them, I felt really embarrassed. There was still some more regarding this. When I told Gus some years later that I was planning a trip back to Japan, he said he wanted to accompany me. So I said to him he could not come. When he asked me why, I told him that he had already died and I had accepted condolence money for him. He looked rather surprised to hear that, but he did not complain.[27] When my brother and sister visited me a few years ago from Japan, I wondered what I should do about Gus. Since it was too difficult to explain everything to them during their short visit, I decided to stick to my previous story. I always kept my youngest son's photo next to my bed so I managed to find Gus's and placed his photo frame next to my son's. I did that before my brother and sister arrived in Adelaide so that they should not be puzzled not to find photos of them side by side. After they went back to Japan, I apologised to Gus's photo and put it away from my bedside.

It took me almost two years before I could sort myself out after the separation. It was difficult for me to accept the relationship which had lasted for forty years could actually end so simply. I had always believed the tie between us was much stronger than that. During that period, I wanted to get back with Gus, although nobody agreed with me. My children did not think their father was a person worth living with. I asked for opinions from Gus's friends, but they also told me to leave him. Poor Gus, he was not respected by anybody at all. Yet, at the same time, nobody, even Gus's brothers, was willing to talk to him to change his mind. They said it was a matter between him and me. If this was in Japan, someone in the family or a friend would play the role of mediator. However, in Australia, such a matter should be left between husband and wife. It is very different.

As I said, I used to hate him and curse him soon after the separation. However, after almost two years, I finally realised that the hatred would just hurt nobody but myself and would not do anything productive. The teaching of Sōka Gakkai helped me a lot during that period. Whenever I read books and magazines published by Sōka Gakkai, I jot down some sentences which I want to remember in my notebook. Something which could not be solved by myself can be solved after reading some of the teachings. Once I realised that hatred would not bring about a solution, I could think otherwise and started to enjoy myself again.

Around that time, I wrote an essay in Japanese about my life in order to let my children know why their mother had come to Australia and how she coped in this country. Since I could not write in English, I wrote it in Japanese and found somebody to translate it for me. I paid $500 for the translation. It was a big amount of money for me, but I wanted my children to read it. I know the essay was circulated among my children, but nobody said anything about it to me.

This essay was the one which I received in the mail soon after I met Michi in 1993. It was a long and well-written essay. Her handwriting also indicated that Michi was well educated and used to writing. When I was in Adelaide, I asked Sumiko if all the children read the essay and how they reacted to it. After assuring me that all of them read it straight away, she gave me her reaction to the essay from the daughter's point of view. She said, "It was a sad story. I felt I finally knew what had been going on in the family. But I do not think I personally could have done anything differently to change the situation under those circumstances."

Presently, I live in a townhouse in Adelaide on my own. My children keep regular contact with me and help me with various things. It was hard to bring up so many children, but now I feel lucky to have them. They are concerned about my well-being and ring me up now and then to make sure I am all right. Actually, some think I still do not understand sufficient English. It is true that I cannot read much English and have problems understanding it, but I can get by. I read through women's magazines so I am well informed about what the film stars are up to. Recently, I have come to think that if people cannot make themselves understood to me in English, they should go and learn Japanese instead of expecting me to speak in perfect English. The other day, Sumiko's husband phoned me and asked me to recommend a good Japanese restaurant. So I told him the name of a restaurant. When Sumiko heard about the conversation, she was so surprised that her husband could understand my English. It was not a problem for me at all. Why should it be?

Recently, I started to realise that the way I brought my children up was not the same as in an Australian family. I can see that when I look at my grandchildren. My sons' children who have Australian mothers are different from my daughters' children. My sons' children would come to me for kisses and hugs from an early age, but my daughters' children do not do that naturally. I guess I did not do that when my children were small, so they do not do that to their children either. Yet, Frances tells her daughter to kiss me when I leave and the girl protests by saying, "You never kiss your mother, Mum. Why should I do that?"

War bride conventions

I attended the war brides' convention in Melbourne in 1993 for the first time with about fifteen women from Adelaide. I was the first one who heard about the plan from Miyuki in Melbourne and let others know about it at a BCOF reunion. In Adelaide, the women had started to get together regularly because we had more spare time to enjoy ourselves. We usually meet once a month at a Japanese restaurant to enjoy food and chat. Somebody named this group the Kasasagi-kai (Magpie Group). It is not easy to pronounce the name in Japanese, but I heard magpies are the symbol of Adelaide. For the Melbourne convention, we practised a Japanese folk dance and performed it after the meeting for entertainment. That was the first time we ever did something like that in costumes, and it was a lot of fun.

The network among Japanese war brides in the United States and Australia started to take shape in the late 1980s and in the early 1990s. The first convention in Australia was held in 1993 in Melbourne to celebrate the fortieth anniversary of the war brides' arrival in Australia. About ninety women, some with their husbands, attended the occasion from all over Australia. In 1994, the first international convention for war brides was held in Honolulu, Hawaii. About 300 participants came to attend the convention from various parts of the United States and Australia. The second international convention was held in Japan at the old castle town of Aizu-Wakamatsu in 1997 and the third in 1999 in Los Angeles. The fourth convention is going to be held at a Japanese hot springs resort, Beppu, in 2002.

I really enjoyed attending the Melbourne convention. We had all been internalising the feeling of being war brides, so we could share our feelings straight away. I cannot find such empathy with younger Japanese women even if they are married to Australians. I could relate to the women at the convention much more easily because I could assume all of us had married soldiers. I could catch up with those whom I did not see for many years at the convention. One still lives in Sydney and I had not seen her since I left Sydney. Those who attended the convention really had a good time. Others who missed the occasion regretted that they were not there.

In 1994, I attended the Hawaii convention which was organised by the Nikkei International Marriage Association. I had a great time there as well. You asked me if I felt comfortable with those women who moved to America. All of us did. Yes, I felt something in common with them although I had never met them before. We were about the same age and they too had all married soldiers. We all remember the period in Japan when we met our husbands. So naturally, I felt close to them. I did not hesitate to ask their names and start conversations. We usually started our conversations by saying, "We have all become old women, but we used to be so pretty when we were young, weren't we?" We talked about our time in Japan before we left, by asking where we used to live in Tokyo and other things. We mainly talked about the time we were in Japan. I did not feel any big difference between the women from America and those of us from Australia. Although they might pronounce some English words with different accents, it did not matter because we all spoke in Japanese.

The term "war bride" [sensō hanayome]

"Sensō hanayome" is a literal translation of the English words "war bride". However, those two terms in the two languages have different connotations. The English term "war bride" might evoke old-fashioned love stories between American soldiers and Australian girls during World War II, while the Japanese translation, "sensō hanayome", is a more tricky phrase for Japanese

to use.[28] It has almost a derogatory connotation and can be demeaning. In the Japanese media, the women are often described as "so-called sensō hanayome" [iwayuru sensō hanayome]. By inserting "so-called", the media tries to separate a particular woman from the stigma which has been attached to the term. But simultaneously, the media draws attention to the stain carried by the term and places the woman in the historical context of post-war Japan.

The unsympathetic attitudes of the general public in Japan toward the relationships between the occupation soldiers and the Japanese women have already been made apparent in the previous chapters. In that period, any level of personal relationship between Japanese women and occupation soldiers was not readily approved. The women were often scorned and abused as traitors and seen as loose women, but at the same time envied because of their access to an abundance of goods through their boyfriends. The women's willingness to mix with foreign soldiers was often suspected as being materially driven. And this motivation became a source of their condemnation.

Many Japanese women who married foreign soldiers refuse to be called "sensō hanayome" and are offended by the term because of its stigma. As the women are aware of the stigma, they try hard to remove themselves from the sensō hanayome category even though they are happy to admit that they are married to Australians. Instead, they want to define themselves as internationally married women. I was told various reasons why they were not "sensō hanayome". Some said that they did not meet their husbands during the war, but after the war. Therefore, the word "sensō" [war] should not be applied to them. A woman claimed that she was not a sensō hanayome because her husband was already a civilian when she met him. Although this claim was contested by other war brides, she asserted that her marriage was not to an occupation soldier, but to a civilian. Whatever the reasons the women gave, they denied that they could be accurately categorised as "sensō hanayome".

Michi's perception of the term "sensō hanayome"

I do not mind being called a "sensō hanayome" at all. I believe that it is an accurate description of us because we all married soon after the war. I know some women who do not like this label. It was true that some women who associated with occupation soldiers were from brothels, and some of them might have reached this country as wives. Yet, I would say most of those women who engaged in prostitution did that in order to survive and support their families. In a sense, those women sacrificed themselves for the sake of their families. Yet, people, especially those who had lost their husbands or brothers in the war, looked down on those women and wondered how they could hold the hands of ex-enemies. I remember I used to look down on those women harshly at that time and regarded them as dirty. At the same time, I was annoyed to be categorised with them when I was dating Gus. However, when I look back, that was the springtime of our youth regardless of who we were. That was the best time in our lives. People might have said that the women who were hanging onto the arms of occupation soldiers looked disgraceful, but we were enjoying our happiest days then. We all began to cry after we arrived in our husbands' countries. In our lives, sometimes we laugh and sometimes we cry. So, I don't think we can criticise those women who went out with the soldiers for money. They did not do that just for fun, but because they needed money to survive. Often they had to support their families as well. Since there were virtually no jobs available then, they had to do that in order to feed themselves.

International marriage

The interviews could not be completed without asking Michi about her view on international marriage. She had made the very unconventional decision to marry an Australian serviceman over fifty years ago in the face of family members' opposition and general social disapproval. The decisions led her to the extraordinary circumstances that have been closely followed in this book. Her decision to marry an Australian determined who she is and where she is. At the same time, I wanted to avoid asking her an abrupt question, such as "Was your marriage a happy one?" I believed a question such as this would be too direct and would not provide her with any room for reflection. That was why I adopted an impersonal and hypothetical question which had been put to another war bride about advising a young Japanese woman in international marriage.

This question fortunately provided Michi with a chance to objectify her experiences and to compose answers without making them too personal. At the same time, her answers were strikingly frank and non-evasive appraisals of the situations she had gone through.

Your question to me was what kind of advice I would give when a young Japanese woman who is in love with an Australian man asked me if she should marry him. Well, I do not think international marriage is a good thing, so I would not recommend it to young Japanese women. I had so much hardship for myself for forty years. I would advise them to marry their own countrymen. Of course, marrying a countryman does not guarantee a happy marriage, but, at least, she has friends nearby when things do not go well. On the other hand, we did not have a supportive network among Japanese war brides in Australia. When I had many problems with my husband, I could not tell my Japanese friends about them, because the news would spread through the community quickly. Well, I did tell somebody about my unhappiness when I was in Melbourne. People did not sympathise with me by saying, "Poor thing", but the story became more and more exaggerated within the community. At the end, I was blamed for my own unhappiness and was accused of being the one who caused all the problems. I heard people were saying, "The reason her husband ended up like that was because she did not behave properly." I was hurt badly when I realised what people were saying about me. I vowed not to tell any Japanese about my problems, except Fumiko, my closest friend, whom I trust.

When you have problems, it is a great help if you have somebody with whom you can talk. I learned in a Japanese TV documentary about a Japanese war bride who committed suicide in America. Maybe she did not have anybody to talk to. I thought about suicide sometimes, but I could not do that because of my children. I forgot where we were living then, but my husband once told me to go back to Japan. I could not when I worried about how the children would cope and who would look after them. I was determined to stay with him in order to feed my children. I think I endured all the hardships for my children's sake. I learned about the virtue of perseverance by watching my mother endure hardships. That was why I could persist.

I do not think young women can do the same thing these days. Our generation survived the war in spite of all the hardship. Difficulties did not fall just upon some individuals, but on everybody in society during that period. Since women of our generation had gone through that hard period, we could endure poverty and other problems after we arrived in Australia. I believe those women who went to America experienced similar problems. We all overcame hardship and sadness. If one was overwhelmed by those feelings, one might have committed suicide. These days, a young woman can get a divorce and go back to her own family in Japan. I know somebody who did that recently in Adelaide. She could do that, but we could not. When I look back, I remember I wanted to go back to Japan with my children when everything was too difficult. I would have done if I did not need to cross the ocean and if I could have walked back. Maybe I withstood the hardship because I did not have any other choice. If I could have hopped on an airplane and arrived back in Japan overnight, I might have left Australia as the young woman did.

In spite of all the problems I have experienced, I am still grateful to Gus for bringing me to Australia. I cannot forget how happy I was to receive the letter from him, which said that he was going to bring the children and myself to Australia. At that time, I loved him dearly and he responded to that by bringing us to this country. How I am now really depends on the decision he made. I do not know how I would be if he had abandoned us then. That is why I keep wondering if I should forgive him and let him come back if he wants to. Yet, if I mention such a feeling to my children, they say, "Mum! Stop it!"

Two years after the main interview sessions, I met Michi again in 1997 in Japan when the second war brides convention was held. She arrived in Japan with Frances and her children a few weeks before the convention started and had a holiday with them. She looked well and happy and told me that Frances bought her a nice cottage and she had moved in there. Gus remarried somebody a few years ago and she was not agonising whether she should let him come back or not any more. At the convention, an essay contest was organised for the war brides by American Airlines. Michi sent in an essay with the title "War, Peace and My Life" and won the first prize, a return ticket between America and Japan. The Association negotiated with the airline to convert the tickets into a money prize so that Michi could use the money to attend the next convention.

The following is an English translation of her essay. Although the essay is relatively long and some sections have already been told in her narrative in this book, it is included here because it is an excellent example of her representation of her life. This was how she wrote her own life in Japanese.

Family get-together at Frances's second wedding in 1994. All of Michi's children except Wayne gathered for the occasion.

War, Peace and My Life

War has been with me since I was born. When I was young, I made countless trips to the train station to cheer departing soldiers with "Banzai" as they were joining the war. As a young woman, I worked for Asahi Film in Tokyo and edited news films. One day, when we were having lunch on the roof top of the office building, a strange-looking airplane with stars on its wings flew in our direction. As it approached the Shinagawa area, we started to hear the sound of anti-aircraft guns. Everything happened very quickly. Later, we heard the plane was the first North American aircraft which came to Japan for a reconnaissance flight. As I worked on news films of the war every day at work, I started to dream of joining the war outside Japan. Luckily, I found a job as a typist in the Ministry of the Navy and was sent to New Guinea as administrative staff for the Civil Government there. A year before the end of the war, all the typists were sent back to Japan from New Guinea. Things were miserable during the war, but similar difficult situations continued after the war. Even now, I cannot forget that a large number of orphans were living in the underpass of Ueno Station as street children. A brother and a sister who were as young as five years old were sleeping on the pavement side by side in rags. Soldiers who were repatriated to Japan from overseas were wearing clothes stained with dirt and sweat. I could tell their clothes were infested with lice. People now joke that it took so many days to get rid of the lice from their bodies.

A few years later, foreign soldiers were driving around the town in their jeeps. I went to dance at one of the dance halls in order to lighten worries and woes which had settled deep inside me. I met Gus at a dance hall and we eventually got married. I had problems at home as my father wasted the family estate for his own pleasure, and that caused sorrow for my mother. I was attracted to Gus who, with his smattering of Japanese, was nice to women as most foreigners were. Interaction with him relieved my melancholy. Some time later, we started to live together. As marriages between Australian soldiers and Japanese women were not allowed then, I could not formally become his wife for a few years. In the meantime, we had a daughter and a son two years apart. On the day our son was born, Gus was sent to Korea as the Korean War started. He returned to Japan two months later.

In 1952, Gus received an order to be transferred back to Australia. At that time, the marriage was not yet permitted by the Australian Government. He took a piece of paper with the address of my mother, where the children and I would be staying. If he threw away the paper, he would abandon us as well. However, Gus kept the paper in his pocket and went home to his parents in Australia. Soon good news reached us. His letter said that the government recognised the marriage, and his application to bring the children and myself was being processed. My mother repeatedly told me possible problems of living in a far land and difficulty in the new language. At the same time my mother, who was born in the Meiji Era, told me to be a virtuous Japanese woman again and again. I was also hoping to live up to that ideal wholeheartedly.

When we arrived in Sydney after a month-long boat trip, it was night. I finally got together with Gus after a year of separation. I realised my new life would start in a new country. When four of us got together again in a car as he drove us to his parents', I felt I could not be happier in my life. Since I arrived in Australia as his fiancée, we organised an Australian wedding ceremony. We had already lived together for six years and our two children attended the ceremony. I felt as if each of us had already had another marriage.

We moved to an army camp in Darwin where a tropical climate greeted us, and I experienced my first disappointment there. I felt lonely as my husband drank every night and I had to stay up to wait for him well past midnight. I did not have anybody who would listen to my worries and I felt completely isolated as the silence surrounded me. Soon, the third child was born. Our neighbours were all nice to us although I could not understand English so well. One day, when I went into the town for shopping, I visited a fish shop. An old man who was mumbling to himself asked me where I came from. When I answered Japan, he almost grabbed my hands and started to tell me his story. "I used to know a Japanese woman whom I loved. Her name was Yoshiko. She was sent back to Japan as the war broke out. We lost contact and cannot contact by letters. I don't know how she is now. She said she would come back when things became peaceful, but I have been waiting. Peace is here, but not Yoshiko." I cannot forget his sad eyes which were filled with tears. By the time I tried to visit him again, he had passed away. The war brought about separation as well as birth of love. Love also brought sadness, hatred, and happiness. Nationalities affected the outcome of love and influenced people's lives. A woman can devote her life to a love she has found.

By the time I had three children, I realised the place I needed to settle down was Australia. Gus was transferred eleven times in twenty years from camp to camp. Whenever we moved to a new camp, a new baby arrived. "I want to enjoy my own life." That was what Gus used to say, so the children were a nuisance to him. He enjoyed his drinking and womanising and sometimes could not remember how many children he had. He was interested only in himself.

By the time my husband retired from the Army we had seven children. They were not appreciated by their father, but I put my best efforts into nurturing a loving home for them. One day, when we went to a sea-port, I saw a Japanese cargo ship which was moored there. I started to cry when I saw a Japanese flag on the ship. Until then, I did not have time to think about my home country because I was too busy looking after the children. "That is the flag of Japan. Your mummy's home country," I said that to my children as I tried not to cry. They were staring at me without a word.

Difficulty in making a living, sadness, resentment of life, goodness and evil. All these feelings have passed through my life as if they were ever-changing lights in a kaleidoscope. I had contemplated committing suicide now and then. Whenever I touched on the thought, I thought of those hordes of orphans and men in military uniform covered in lice after the war. Those people were working hard to reconstruct Japan. So I should not be defeated and kill myself because of such a minor worry. I should live and make sure my children will realise the dreams that I could not make true. So, in a sense, the war itself provided me with the strength to live.

Forty years had passed. When I was approaching seventy years of age, Gus met a new woman. He did not come home at night. My children suggested we should separate. When I realised my forty years as a war bride had finally come to an end, I could not help but cry. I came to this country as a bride without knowing anybody but Gus. I was hoping to have an ordinary happy family with seven children and fourteen grandchildren. But that was to no avail. I packed my things and left the house. For a woman, separation is more painful than death and more desolate.

I was a war bride who was abandoned at the age of seventy, but I would not be defeated with a broken heart. Joy does not last forever and life shows us different alternatives. So we can choose one or the other and no decision is the correct one. There are continuous obstacles in one's life. When one obstacle is cleared, another appears. Such is one's life, I believe. I would never go backward as long as I live.

My children now make contributions to society and became successful in business. They bought me a house. As I approach eighty years old, I am thankful that I am close to my family and filled with happiness. My ex-husband is seeing another woman even though his health is declining. If that is what he enjoys doing in his life, let it be so. I do not object. Yet, whenever he finds a new woman, my heart sinks and saddens. As I am happy now, I hope he is happy as well.

In a novel *Hōrōki*, Fumiko Hayashi wrote as follows:

"Happiness for a woman is to love a man, to bear children for him, to nurse him to his death and to be nursed by the children to her own death." I still believe these words describe the ultimate happiness for a woman.

War brides were all young and pretty forty years ago. As dandelion seeds travel a long distance in the wind, war brides migrated to foreign countries. They persevered in isolation, and withstood financial difficulties. They are now rooted in the country where they arrived and are producing flowers. When I reflect upon our past, each of us experienced ups and downs and created our own dramas of life. Even the wrinkles on our faces were the evidence of our hard work.

Death will finish everything. Wherever he is, it is good to know that Gus is still alive. I wish him health and happiness.

I pray for world peace from a corner in Australia. Once I read the following words: "Those who are in their sixties and seventies are at their best. When the invitation from the other world arrives in your eighties and nineties, send it back and make them wait till you reach one hundred." (Translated by Tamura)

Michi (left) at the Migration Museum in Adelaide with Mrs Sadako Morris (centre) and the author (right) in October 2000. An exhibition on war brides was held at the museum between September and November 2000.

Chapter Five
Children's Views

MICHI AND GUS had seven children, two daughters and five sons, who were born between 1948 and 1960. They were Sumiko, George, Wayne, Frances, Robert, William and Ronald in order of birth. Out of those, six survive as the youngest son, Ronald, committed suicide in 1981. I interviewed four of them. Interviews with Sumiko, Frances and William were carried out in Adelaide in November 1999, and with George in Perth in September 2000. The other two, Wayne and Robert, could not be interviewed because of distance and their work commitments. Sumiko was the first child, born in Japan. She lived in Adelaide and worked for her husband's business. As she said herself, she was a quiet person who seemed to possess strength of mind within herself. She preferred to be called Sam instead of Sumiko or Sumi for the reasons I will discuss later in this chapter. George was also born in Japan as the second child and eldest son. He lived in Perth and became successful in his own business. When I interviewed him, he had just sold his business and was contemplating a career change. Frances was the fourth and younger daughter. She was an outgoing and sociable woman who used to work as a model when she was young. She ran a motel with her husband. William was the youngest surviving child. He worked as a bank manager in Adelaide City and was a dedicated husband and father to his young family. All of them maintained regular contact with Michi at a day-to-day level and played important roles in Michi's present life. Frances visited her mother most frequently and made sure everything was fine for her. Sam also visited her mother as much as she could, but not as regularly as Frances. The two daughters seemed to take up the main responsibility of making sure Michi was well looked after. William visited Michi on weekends with his wife and three young children. Michi's other three sons, including George, lived interstate, but they maintained regular contact with their mother over the phone. It was quite clear to me that the children were concerned about Michi and tried to do their best to keep her happy.

When I approached the children through Michi for interviews in November 1999 they were happy to cooperate. Previously, I had met Sam and Frances in 1995 and had talked with them briefly about their mother, but I had not had a chance to interview them formally. The 1999 interviews in Adelaide took place on a weekend at Michi's house. The interview with George was carried out at his residence in Perth with his wife Isabelle present, while I was visiting the city for a conference.

Previously, all the children had read Michi's own essay, which was written soon after her separation from Gus. This essay covered the period from the time she met Gus in Japan until her separation from him after forty years of marriage. It was written firstly in Japanese and later translated into English at Michi's own expense so that the children could read it and understand why their mother came to Australia. She felt she had not had much chance to talk about that with her children. She was expecting to receive some feedback afterwards, but none of them gave their responses to her, which was rather disappointing for her. Consequently, she suggested I ask about their reaction to her essay when I was going to talk with her daughters in 1995. Sam's response was, "Yes, everybody read the essay straight away." When she was asked her reaction to it, she answered, "It was a sad story. But I could not do anything to change the situation." From her words, I could sense she read it from her own personal perspective and tried to figure out where in the story she would fit in. When I asked a similar question of Frances in 1995, she did not say much to me either. When I asked George about the essay in 2000, he said he did not "feel any great emotion" after reading the essay. He was surprised that his mother wrote the essay and had it translated into English, but he only thought his mother was trying to "prove something or justify herself".

The second life story of Michi which the children read was the one I wrote for my PhD thesis. Prior to the recent interviews, Michi distributed copies to her children. I also translated it into Japanese so that Michi could read what I wrote. The period that my work covered was longer than her own essay, as the story started in Japan before the war. None of the children knew Michi was once engaged to a Japanese naval officer who was killed in the war. They did not know that she was in New Guinea during the war, either. The children's reactions to the story were very positive and all of them said that they enjoyed reading it. However, how they each related to the story turned out to be quite different.

This difference became apparent when I asked each of them if she/he agreed to the publication of the story in English using their real names. Previously, I had a discussion with Michi about publishing her story as a book and she was quite keen to have her story published in English for the sake of her family who did not read or speak Japanese. George, Frances and William said that they did not have any objections as long as their mother was happy with the arrangement. George even said he would prefer to appear under his real name rather than with a pseudonym because the story was a true story. They also said they were excited to read about their mother before and during the Pacific War, especially her engagement to a naval officer and her experience in New Guinea. In contrast, Sam expressed her reservations indirectly. Although she would not object to the publication, she was not sure if she would be happy to appear in the book under her real name. When I asked her if she felt rather hesitant to publication of a book itself, she answered:

> Yes, I am a little bit. I mean, it is Mum's story so it is not for me to say. [But] I say it is such a personal thing. I personally would not like to use my real identity, but it is Mum's story. So if that is what she is happy to do, then it is OK. It is not my decision to say. Only because it is very personal.

Later, she formally contacted me to say that she would prefer to have a pseudonym in this book. Thus, the name I am using in this book to refer to her is not her real name. In spite of repeating that the story was her mother's story, Sam could not read it from a distance as the other brothers and sister did. In addition, Sam commented that she did not find anything new in my rendering of her mother's life story.

> But what you wrote about Mum, because I've known her and read her story that she wrote years and years ago, it was all the same sort of story. I think I know all of this. It is just the same story

going over and over again. Every time Mum writes it is always the same. It is really nothing new to me. Mum is hoping for some sort of reaction from me, but it was hard for me to give that. Because, I said to her, it is the same story ... I guess when she writes another story it will be the same again. It is the same thing over and over again. I guess it is not creating an impact on me. Whereas it might have done to Frances and even to Bill [William] because it might be the first time they actually came across it and actually understood and read it. Whereas for me, I have read the story so many times. (laugh) Like reading the same book year after year.

I could sense a certain level of resentment in Sam's words due to the fact that she was expected to give some type of feedback to Michi and myself. For George, Frances and William, Michi's story was their mother's story, but at the same time, it was a fascinating story which they could appreciate with curiosity and interest. On the other hand, since her childhood Sam was deeply involved in Michi's life. Thus, she did not need to be reminded again and again by either her mother or myself. This reaction of Sam's proved to be an indicator of how much she was influenced by Michi's life. As Sam and her mother had gone through her mother's experience together, she knew the story well enough and reading Michi's life stories did not give her any fresh insight. As Sam's reaction to Michi's story was the most intense, I am going to focus on her perceptions of experiences with her mother in this chapter.

Sam's childhood

Sam was born in Japan in 1948 as the first child of Michi and Gus. It is probably true to say that her birth cemented the relationship between them. Sam's photo as a toddler showed a blond Eurasian girl with a determined look. She acknowledged that she did not have strong Asian features since she was young, and even now, it is difficult to detect that she has Asian heritage in her blood. According to Sam, it helped her not having strong Asian features. In contrast, her younger brother, Robert, had much more distinctive Asian features, and Sam and other siblings commented that Robert had often got into fights with other children probably because of his different looks.

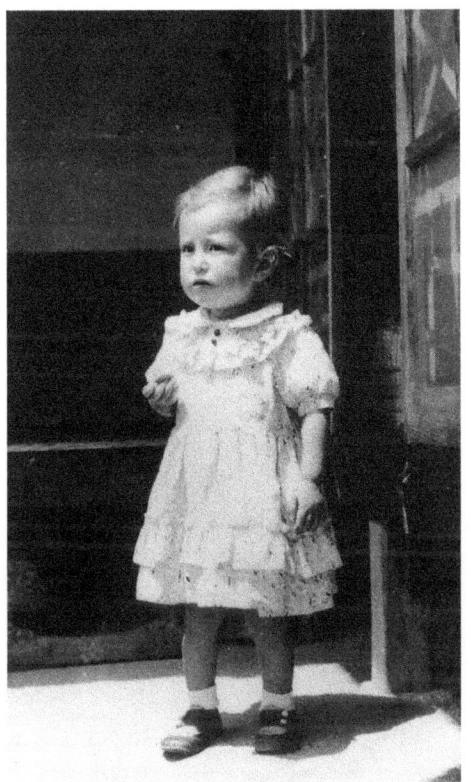

Two-year-old Sumiko at her grandmother's house in Tokushima.

However, Sam still faced some big problems while she was growing up. The first one was that she often needed to move to different schools due to her father's transfers. She recalled the difficulties she encountered, but also displayed a positive attitude towards the experience.

> My whole schooling was difficult. The biggest problem, I guess, was the fact that we were moving all the time. You just make friends and then you move to a new place and start all over again … I always had those problems even in high school. Once I got established it was good in one way because it made me very strong.

George also recalled that he found it hard to adjust to new schools and new systems after each shift. He admitted that he struggled academically at school mainly because of this demand of constant readjustment and he had to wait until he started to work as an apprentice to learn his trade before he became more confident in himself. For Sam, as she excelled in both academic and sporting aspects at school, she found it easier to make friends in a new environment:

> I was lucky in a way because I was always capable at school. And very good at sport. That made me a bit of a leader. I guess that

helped. Because I was good at everything, people wanted to become friends with me. I still was a sort of a shy person, but being good at sport and all that, helped me to lift me above that … If I weren't, it would have been very hard for me because I would have got picked on a lot.

Name "Sumiko"

Yet, she had another major problem and that was her unusual first name. Her real name was Sumiko. It was a common name in Japan, but a very unusual name in Australia when she was growing up. She frankly admitted that having a Japanese first name caused problems for her when she was young. It was a "funny name" for her.

> I had a lot of problems with that. I got to a stage where I used to almost get angry with my parents for giving me a funny name. Because it just made it hard for me. That was always just an issue when I had to try making friends. Once that was established, it was OK. Yeh. It was very hard. From primary right through to high school.

Sam continued:

> If I did not have an Asian name, it would have been a little bit easier. Because people say, "What is your name? What is your name?" When you told them what your name is, "What!" "What sort of name is that?" Partly because I didn't look very Japanese, if I didn't have an Asian name, it would have been a little bit easier because people would not react like that. Because I have a funny name, "Oh! Where do you come from?" Then you have to tell them a whole background. "I was born in Japan. Mother is Japanese" and all this. You have to give almost the whole history to everybody. To every new person you meet.

When she was asked to explain about her name, she was constantly reminded of the tie between herself and Japan through her mother. Contemporary Australians are more tolerant of cultural and racial diversity, but in the 1950s being different from the rest was not something people, especially children, appreciated. Thus, the frequent explanations she had to give regarding her name inevitably made her very self-conscious of her background.

Sam commented that the situation had not changed much even now, though she finds it much easier to explain about her own background as an adult. She decided to shorten her name and she preferred to be called "Sam".

> I still get it now when I am introduced to new people. "Oh, Sam." I shortened my name just to Sam. "Is that from Samantha?" "No, it is from Sumiko" "That is unusual. What is that?" "Japanese." "How come you've got a Japanese name?" "OK. My mother is Japanese" and so on. Now that I am an adult, it is easier. I don't have any problems with it. It is still, I have to give some explanation to anybody that is new. I still have that as far as my name is concerned. I don't have any problems with it, but as a child I did. It just made it so difficult.

That was why Sam expressed her strong opposition when Frances wanted to name her first daughter Sumiko. Sam tried to discourage her sister from giving the name to her daughter because she did not want her niece to go through the same experience she had had. However, Frances insisted because she "liked the name" and named her daughter Sumiko. According to Frances, the young Sumiko had some problems with her first name, but she was not affected as much as her aunt was.

The eldest child

As the eldest of seven and the first daughter, Sam was expected to help her mother and did so even when she was very young. She also played the role of a second mother to her younger siblings. George, who is a few years younger than Sam, remembered that she was determined to make all the siblings walk back from school even though some of them complained of the heat and tiredness. By assisting her mother, Sam knew first-hand the various difficulties Michi had experienced as a Japanese woman who was rearing a big family, without much help from her husband, and not knowing the language and culture of the country. In this sense, Michi's Japanese background affected not only the mother but also the daughter. On the other hand, the younger children were not involved as intensely as Sam in Michi's day-to-day life probably because Sam took care of things. Thus, Frances stated that the fact her mother was Japanese made no difference to her when she was growing up. Similarly, William recalled that as one of the youngest of the seven, he felt much closer to his elder brothers, particularly to George, than to his parents.

Sam was four years old when she arrived in Australia and started preschool in Darwin. Michi remembered Sam learned English fast and adapted to the Australian way of life very quickly. At a very young age, Sam started to act as an interpreter for her mother at the doctor's when her siblings got sick. When Michi and Gus went out to parties in the Camp, she babysat the rest of the children. At school as well, she made sure her younger siblings were all right and not bullied.

> I remembered having to look after them and when I heard anything about somebody picking on them, I was running down to find out what was going on. I don't remember bashing anybody, I would come close to it a few times. Given a few threats. I never got physical. I know that. I don't remember hitting anybody over it or fighting over it. I remembered having a few strong words with people, "Don't pick on them any more. If you say that again, you can deal with me" type of thing. But that was all just early days when they started primary school, but after that, I don't remember ever having to fight any wars for them or worry about them.

In contrast to Sam, Frances did not encounter any problems at school. She said:

> Nobody made any difference with me. No one made any silly comments. No. It did not affect me very much. Not that I can remember, anyway.

For Frances, having a Japanese mother did not affect her.

> There is a big [age] difference between Sam and I, but I don't remember it [having a Japanese mother] ever affected me so much. I don't think people looked at me and thought I had a Japanese mother. They did not know my nationality. Some people picked it up, but not a lot of people did. No, it did not affect me at all.

Frances said that people generally find it difficult to identify her ethnic background. She said sometimes people thought she was Mexican.

She had an exotic attractiveness and she used to do modelling when she was young. In her case, the Eurasian features were a positive factor. The contrasting experiences and perception between Sam and Frances were partly because of their personality differences: Sam's reserved character and Frances' easygoing character. Secondly, birth order in the family must have influenced them. Sam took the main responsibility to look after Michi and the family as the eldest, while Frances did not need to get involved as a younger member of the family. Also, at school, people were already used to the children of the family by the time Frances and the younger brothers started school. Lastly, it is possible to say there was a shift in Australian society towards multiculturalism by the time Frances was growing up. As the number of non-British immigrants increased in the fifties and sixties, having non-Anglo-Celtic background was not as big a stigma as when Sam was young.

For Sam, her Japanese mother brought a Japanese first name and the necessity to assist her mother with day-to-day matters. In addition, Sam was expected to give emotional support when her mother encountered marriage and family problems. At the end, Sam had to be responsible not only for herself and the other children, but for her mother's welfare. It was painful for Sam not to realise what was actually going on between her parents until she was much older. As she recalled, she was there and witnessed some incidents, but she did not then know what they meant or why they were happening.

> I probably did not understand what was happening. Or knew about it. Probably wasn't until years later. When I think back now, I did not understand fully until first I read Mum's story. Yeh, I remembered that. I remembered that happening. Now I understand why that was happening. At the time, probably I was just too young to understand.

Sam seemed to think that she should have been more helpful to her mother when those incidents were happening. At the same time, she knew that it would be unreasonable to expect a young girl to comprehend the situation fully.

> I don't think Mum fully understands the fact of the age I was when these things were happening. I think that because she is older, I don't think she stops and thinks I would have been too young to help ... Even I have to stop and remind myself that I was actually

five years old, eight years old and ten years old. (voice becomes teary) I am thinking I should have done this and I should have done that. Then I am thinking, "No, hang on. You were tiny. What could you do?" ... At the time, there could not be anything I could have done. Because something happened so long ago, you sort of tend to forget. The age of the person involved and the circumstances.

I was concerned whether the way Gus was depicted in Michi's narrative was fair to him and asked Sam and George, the two eldest children, who knew more about their parents' relationship. Both of them agreed that the way Michi talked about her husband was fairly accurate. George described his father as "immature" and somebody who never grew up. Thus, he was more interested in himself than his family. When the parents finally decided to separate, George said the children were all relieved and supported Michi financially and emotionally. None of the children took the father's side. Yet, George maintained a tie with his father through occasional phone calls and visits. Sam also said that she did not hate him because of how he treated her mother and the children. Both claimed that their father was not a good father in terms of his selfishness, but he never became abusive or violent. As Sam said, "He put a roof over our heads and food on the table." Yet, there does not exist the emotional closeness between him and the children as exists with their mother.

Another difficulty for Sam was the communication problem. By observing her mother for many years, Sam was aware that Michi nodded and signalled her agreement even when she did not fully understand what was being said. Michi commented to me about her habit in the interview with me and said she somehow instinctively knew what was being said even though she could not follow each sentence. Sam commented on this:

> Sometimes, I don't think she fully understands what people are saying. Not just me, even other people. Because she is used to saying, "Yes, Yes, I know what you are talking about." When she is talking to English people, unless you respond, they are not going to say any more. Hard for them to try to explain. Therefore, it is easier for her just to nod her head and say yes, that's right and go along with it even though she may not fully understand what they say. I know she does that all the time. Quite a bit.

However, such type of automatic affirmation was dangerous when the discussion concerned emotional matters in the family relationship. Due to Michi's lack of English to express herself, Sam said she had to guess. Not only that, when she talked to Michi, she was not sure whether her mother fully understood her or not. Michi sometimes did misunderstand Sam and became upset. Sam did not realise the misunderstanding had occurred until her mother complained to another member of the family, usually Frances. Only after Frances contacted Sam to express her concern did Sam realise that Michi did not fully understand what Sam had said to her.

> Half of the time, you don't know she misunderstood, you know. It might come out accidentally when she may say something to somebody else. Then, they get back to me. "No, I didn't say that." Yes, there is still a language barrier between us and it is a bit difficult.

Sam admitted that the language problem which existed between Michi and herself affected their mother–daughter relationship while she was growing up.

> We couldn't have close talks. Yeh. When I think back over the years, when I was young and growing up with Mum, we never had that close mother–daughter thing. I mean because of the language. I am sure because of the language problem. She was supportive of me and I was very supportive of her because of the problems she had. But we never had that real closeness of being able to help each other. Because she could not let me know exactly how she felt. Nor could I converse back to her and say, "This is how it affected me." You got to a stage where I had to try and fight my own problems without dragging her into it. So to try to help out as much as I can that way ... Anything I had to deal with, I tried to deal with myself rather than go running to her. Whereas in most other families, daughters would go straight to the mother and say, "I've got a problem. Can you help me?" I could not do that.

Her reaction at that time was frustration at not understanding and not being understood.

> I can remember a lot of the times I felt angry about the situation. A lot of times, I felt "Why is this happening to me?" You know.

That is the sort of things. You can stay around for a long time, but I remember having moments. Thinking "Ah" [a sigh of desperation]. That sort of thing did not really affect me in the long run, so to speak. It is not something I felt bitter about or hurt for years. It was just moments. I felt I was deprived, I guess.

In contrast, the other children did not seem to think there was any problem in communication with their mother. I asked George on this point and he denied any problem by giving regular telephone conversations he had with Michi as an example. In those conversations, they generally exchanged news in the family rather than discussed complicated and emotional matters. In this sense, George, Frances and William took it for granted that Michi's English was imperfect and they did not expect to have more heart-to-heart conversations with their mother while Sam once wanted to reach such a level with her mother.

Now, Sam has come to terms with the past problems and dealt with them positively.

> We are a close family anyway. Still just a bit difficult. That to get to the true nitty-gritty of how we feel because it is very hard to express that. We just have to show her, I guess. You cannot do anything about it and you cannot actually talk about it. I guess we never did that when we were younger, as far as expressing ourselves, probably we don't do it now.

> We are not going to suddenly start talking and having mother–daughter conversations around the table and start talking about how we really feel about this and that. We didn't do it back then, so it will not suddenly start. We are older. As far as the closeness and supportiveness, because Mum went through so much I guess, we are now in the position that we can help her more by being supportive, financially as well as with ourselves, and we can look after her more now. We can show our support now. We can help each other anyway without having to start being a bit more talkative about it, I guess. We don't have to actually say things. We know that we help each other and support each other. We don't actually have to say that.

The initial hesitant response of Sam when she was told of the publication proposal of this book led me to explore how she related to her mother's life story. The rest of her brothers and sister regarded Michi's story basically as their mother's story and could read it with a certain level of detachment as they discovered her past which was not known to them previously. In contrast, Sam's involvement in Michi's life was the longest and the most intense. It was not easy for her to enjoy reading her life story with the same level of detachment. Sam knew the story was not only her mother's story of establishing a place in Australia but also her own experience of being accepted as an Australian in the 1950s and 1960s. Sam's dedication to her mother and family from a young age was clearly evident in her narrative as she had to play a crucial role. At the same time, her narrative revealed the pain she endured with her mother and also by herself.

Epilogue
Personal Reflections – Keiko Tamura

I CAME BACK to Australia in 1990 after three years of academic nomadic life, which took my family and myself to Japan and Germany as my physicist husband moved with his jobs. We had two young children and did not have much money, as shifting from one country to another depleted our savings. I was determined to do a PhD degree in anthropology, but I desperately needed an appropriate topic. While we were in Japan, I carried out preliminary research on the Ainu and their craft industry by visiting Hokkaido. At that time, the Ainu craft industry and tourism seemed to be an interesting topic as it would be an extension of my MA thesis on the Aboriginal craft industry in Central Australia. However, by the time we came back to Australia, I realised I could not pursue the original topic because fieldwork in Hokkaido would involve another uplifting of my family from Australia. Furthermore, living costs in Japan would be too expensive for those who needed to support themselves with the weak Australian dollar.

I searched for a topic which did not require long-term fieldwork in a remote place. I felt I could not cope with more moving and raising two young boys without my husband's involvement. Around that time, Dr Nicolas Peterson, who had been patiently acting as my supervisor throughout my nomadic and baby-producing years, mentioned to me a documentary film on Japanese war brides. He had not seen it, but he heard it was good and the title included words such as cherry ripe and tea. The term "war brides" did not grab my attention straight away. I knew some of them previously, but they did not seem to be a particularly interesting group of women to me. I recalled an occasion when a war bride talked about her past experience soon after I had arrived in Australia in the early 1980s. She told my Japanese friend and

I that it had taken more than twenty days by boat to travel to Australia. She could not buy soy sauce in Australia so she had to mix water with Vegemite and use it as a substitute. Upon hearing those stories, I remember that my friend and I looked at each other with amazement. Even twenty years ago, direct overnight flights were already in service between Japan and Australia, and Japanese food had started to become more readily available in the country. I did not find much in common with their experience. Thus, the research prospects of Japanese war brides seemed to be similar to studying antiquities, and not very appealing.

However, I thought I should see the film before I decided, and went to the National Library to view the 1989 film *Green Tea and Cherry Ripe* which was directed by Solrun Hoaas. In a small theatrette, I watched the documentary and was struck by the energy each woman was emitting on screen. I soon realised they were not just aging women who were talking about the boat trips to Australia and scarcity of Japanese food as reminiscences. I could sense that their lives in Japan and Australia in the past four decades were evident in the Japanese and English they spoke, and in the way they looked and behaved. I realised I had finally found my thesis topic.

Although the topic was decided, the research did not progress substantially for another two years. With a part-time job and family commitments, I could only keep a small flame of my research interest burning. However, I managed to talk about my intention to Mrs Teruko Blair, a war bride whom I met when I used to work as a tour guide for Japanese tourists. Teruko was very encouraging and assisted me to meet other war brides. We went to a British Commonwealth Occupation Forces national meeting which was held in Canberra. At a dinner after the meeting, I met a group of war brides for the first time.

In 1993, I obtained a postgraduate scholarship and resigned from my part-time job to commence a PhD at The Australian National University as a full-time student. The research finally started to move forward. It was very lucky for me that war brides had started to form networks in Australia and the United States a few years before, and the first ever convention of war brides in Australia was planned that year. Before asking for permission to attend the convention as an observer, I tried to meet some of them informally. The chance came as war brides in Melbourne gathered for their bi-monthly luncheon at a Japanese restaurant, but I felt I could not turn up on my own to introduce myself. Mrs Chiaki Foster who lived in Albury came to the rescue and kindly offered to take me there. She had been living in this inland country town for over thirty years. She was also one of the main characters in the film *Green Tea and Cherry Ripe*. First, I travelled to Albury by bus to meet Chiaki there. I stayed overnight with her and travelled to Melbourne by train the next day for the luncheon meeting.

I still remember how nervous I felt when I arrived at the restaurant, and faced a roomful of women in their sixties. One odd factor which made me very uneasy was that the women looked Japanese, but did not behave like the Japanese women I knew. Their voices were strong and their bodily gestures were more Australian than Japanese. I wondered how I should relate to them, either as Japanese or as Australians. They did not fit into any category I knew. I was there to observe them, but they were observing me as well. I felt intensely self-conscious about what I said and asked. I was worried they might regard me as an intrusive person who wanted to find out about their past. I realise now that, in spite of my best intentions, I had the suspicion that some of them must have had a shady past in Japan which they did not want to reveal.

At the luncheon, I joined a table with Chiaki and tried to have friendly chats with other women in spite of my nervousness. Although I was very self-conscious, they were relaxed and not guarded towards me. Some expressed interest in my research topic, and some did not. However, the words of one woman stuck with me for the rest of my research period. When she heard that my study was about the war brides, she said, "Whether a war bride could lead a happy life in Australia or not all depended on her husband's attitude towards his work and nothing else." I could see there was some truth in her words, but I also wondered if that was all there was. If her happiness completely depended on her husband, her fate had already been determined before she came to Australia. I wanted to explore whether and how she could change her life course through her own initiatives. And my research commenced at last.

It was lucky for me that the research started in 1993. The first convention of Japanese war brides in Australia was held in Melbourne in

1993. The first international convention of Japanese war brides was then held in Hawaii in 1994. This new development provided my research with more dimensions, as I could include information I gathered through participant observation of those activities as well as through historical research. Thus, my research was dealing not only with the war brides' past but also with their present. Inevitably, I soon realised that their present activities were closely connected to their past.

Although historical research and participant observation were important parts of the research, my main focus was on the life history interviews I carried out with the women. I taped twelve life histories, and interviewed more than forty women about various aspects of their lives during my research. Each life history interview was loosely structured although I had a list of questions I wanted to cover. I went back to those women who lived in Canberra as many times as necessary until I could cover all the questions I prepared. With other women, such as Michi, who lived away from Canberra, interviews needed to be carried out in a more intensive form. I often stayed at the war brides' houses when I visited them for interviews, so that we could spend many hours, including evenings, talking about their lives. After some hours of interviews, both of us became exhausted and we decided to have a break and enjoy dinner or cups of tea. Then the topic went back to the issues we were discussing in the interviews and I needed to push the recording button of the tape recorder again.

I did not realise how difficult it was to interview somebody until I actually started. I used to think I was quite good at listening, but I soon realised listening passively and interviewing actively were quite different matters. I organised two trial interviews, one with Teruko since I knew her very well, and another with a daughter of a war bride. At the beginning of those trials, I constantly felt I was violating their privacy by asking intrusive questions. In addition, to keep track of my questions without interrupting the flow of their narratives was mentally exhausting. Eventually, I realised I could not expect an informant to provide me with relevant information unless I asked, and the awkward feeling on my side gradually disappeared. As long as a question was within an appropriate context, an interviewee was quite willing to answer frankly even though it covered sensitive matters. However, the art of steering back the women's narratives along my list of questions was more difficult to master. I still felt exhausted after conducting a few hours of interviews towards the end of my research even though I had become more experienced.

What I gained in my research process was not only the skill of in-depth interviewing. I had a lot of fun as well. Firstly, I managed to get to know so many people in meaningful ways. They became "alive" to me as I learned about their reasons and emotions through the interviews. They were not those who lived completely different lives in different times from me any more. As I learned the social and historical background of their times, their actions and decisions started to make sense to me.

The biggest excitement of all for me was that I was able to explore the war brides' experiences with them. Some of the experiences and emotions they told me had never been revealed to anybody before. At the beginning of interview sessions, women often said that they could not remember the past so well. Some even declared it was their principle to forget about the past. However, as interviews proceeded, they were surprised how much they remembered. Some of the memories came back to them so vividly, it was sometimes disturbing to them. The process of remembering was a joint venture which was carried out through the dialogues between the women and myself. None of them talked about their experiences as a monologue to a tape recorder. At the same time, the interviews were not carried out in the form of an interrogation. I felt I participated and contributed in their rediscovery of their past as a co-explorer.

In the process of analysing their life histories, one aspect proved to be striking. That was the contrast between the ordinary and the extraordinary. When we see the war brides' life course simply as a process of aging, it is nothing extraordinary. It can be described as follows:

> Young women with an ordinary family background went out to work and fell in love with young men. The families expressed concern about their future, but they persisted and got married. The women left their families and moved to their husbands'. They mainly stayed at home to have children and to raise them. Most of them did not have a professional career and their husbands were not public figures. Now in their late sixties, many of them are widows. With modest levels of financial security, most of them live peaceful lives, enjoying interaction with their grandchildren and their female friends.

In fact, this is the way many of the war brides see themselves. When I approached war brides to ask for interviews, a typical response was: "Why do you want to interview me? I have nothing interesting to tell you. I have led such an ordinary life." One daughter said, "I have never seen my mother as a war bride. She is just a mum to me."

However, such ordinariness transforms into extraordinariness when the trajectory of the women's personal lives is laid over the historical and cultural transitions in Japan and Australia during the last five decades. This transformation is as dramatic as the changes in colour-separated negatives: they are dull and uninteresting on their own, but will suddenly transform into a vivid picture when one is superimposed on top of the other.

There are three separate "negatives" of the war brides' experiences: the dimensions of gender, space and time. Firstly, the war brides' experiences were, at most, women's experience in the context of families, and it is possible to interpret them appropriately only when we note this aspect. Their transition from daughters to young women with independent minds in Japan was followed by their becoming wives and mothers in Australia. Now, many of them are widows. At each stage of their lives, their actions and decisions were carried out not just as individuals with their own will and intentions, but also as female members of families and societies.

Secondly, by crossing the Pacific Ocean from Japan to Australia, they also crossed cultures, races and nations. Their departure from Japan meant their removal from the Japanese way of life. After arriving in Australia, they wholeheartedly put their efforts into adjusting to the new way of life. They also crossed the racial boundary from Asia to Australia where the white European population was dominant. While the women had comfortably belonged to the racial majority in Japan, they could not disappear into the crowd in Australia as the number of Asian migrants was small. Lastly, their migration resulted in their movement from one nation to the other. This was no ordinary crossing, since, as it followed the Pacific war so closely, they faced the difficult task of reconciling national histories. The war brides had to incorporate both sets of histories and search for their own position within them. The shift from one nation to another, in space and allegiance, was obviously complicated by the fact that it was taking place in the immediate post-war period. Some Japanese saw them as joining the enemy while some Australians saw them as still being the enemy.

Finally, the war brides' experiences have spanned almost half a century. During this period, Japan's economy has been transformed from a war devastated state to one of the world's leading economic powers. In parallel with the economic development that has played the key role in this transformation, Japanese society has also rapidly opened up to the outside and presently "internationalisation" has become the vogue word throughout Japanese society. In the meantime, Australia has also transformed from white Australia, with a strong assimilation policy, to multicultural Australia advocating cultural tolerance.

When I started the research project, I was simply happy to find an interesting topic. As time passed, I could identify myself more and more with the situation the war brides were in. As my children got older, they were growing up to be Australians, not Japanese, speaking English and thinking like Australians. That forced me to realise that the basis of my life has shifted from Japan to Australia. It was still possible to visit Japan as often as I wanted, but to go back to Japan permanently became almost impossible. As the rest of my family belonged to Australia, I also belonged to this country. This was exactly the situation the women found themselves in several years after their migration. I felt I developed better empathy with the women's thoughts and emotions when I found myself in a similar position to them.

What I personally learned through my research was how strong individuals could be, in this case women, even when they were isolated from their familiar culture and they needed to adapt to a new culture. For the war brides, they were further expected to raise their family as Australian even though they did not know what an Australian family was like. In their cases, their strength was not expressed in the form of a power display or confrontation. Often the existence of their strength was in the form of resilience. From a bystander's point of view, they might have looked frustratingly passive at a certain stage of their lives, but in the long run, they were patient enough to realise what they really wanted, at least to survive. I wanted to convey this type of strength in this book through Michi's life story.

Some war brides thought this resilience was a characteristic of Japanese women and often they used the term "*Yamato nadeshiko*" to describe themselves. *Yamato* means "pure Japanese" without any foreign influence. *Nadeshiko* is a type of plant which belongs to the *dianthus* genus and has pink flowers in early autumn. Although this term was traditionally used to describe the delicate beauty of Japanese women, in contemporary Japan, "*Yamato nadeshiko*" is generally regarded as old-fashioned and rarely used to praise the virtues of Japanese women. When the war brides employed the term to describe themselves, its attributes were not limited to physical beauty. The term also indicated that Japanese women were flexible but resilient in change, just as the flower might sway in a strong wind but never break. The war brides identified themselves with this particular quality. For many of them, their efforts to assimilate and their achievement in becoming good Australian wives and mothers were a manifestation of Japanese women's characteristics of flexibility. At the same time, they continued to pursue their commitment to marriage and their children as a manifestation of their resilience. Thus, by being adaptable to change as well as doggedly pursuing their initial commitment, they had demonstrated their strength — their delicate strength — as Japanese women.

I am not sure whether such characteristics are particular solely to Japanese women. It could be interpreted as characteristic of women in general, or more broadly as characteristic of human beings. However, almost fifty years after leaving their home country, they have established their own place in Australia and the second and following generations are thriving in this country. By establishing themselves in their adopted country and producing successive generations, they have certainly left their own mark here in this country. This is the proof of their strength.

Endnotes

1 The other three key naval bases were Yokosuka, Sasebo and Maizuru.

2 *Monpe* trousers were made of cotton and worn as working gear in the fields. Women were probably instructed to wear trousers in order to protect their chastity.

3 National Archives of Australia (A5954/1).

4 Australian War Memorial (130/31 [52a]).

5 The Australian War Memorial photographic database contains a photograph of five women who were found to have VD during a periodic medical examination of female employees.

6 The wages for the Japanese workers who were working for BCOF were paid by the Japanese Government.

7 This was an overwhelming sentiment among a group of Japanese men who were ex-BCOF employees when they gathered in January 1994 in Kure for me and discussed their experiences in the camp.

8 According to the Japanese national census in 1947, the number of men between 20 and 29 years old was 5.77 million, while the number of women of the same age group was 6.78 million. Thus, there was a difference of one million. Mrs Teruko Blair remembers that people used to describe the situation in an expression, "A truck-full of women for one young man" (personal communication).

9 Interviews conducted by the author with the Japanese ex-employees of BCOF at Kure in January 1994.

10 *BCOF Bound*, p.10.

11 Australian War Memorial (114/423/10/17).

Endnotes

12 There is no detailed record of how many Japanese women married Australians and migrated to Australia. However, according to Kure City Office records, there were 650 Australian–Japanese couples. Some marriages occurred in Tokyo where BCOF also had a small base. Out of those couples, not all of them moved to Australia. Some stayed in Japan and some others went to Britain. Thus, the number 650 seems to be the most accurate estimate for the number of Japanese war brides who moved to Australia.

13 Mr Robert Wollard was interviewed by the author on 15 September 1997 in Canberra.

14 Ms Yone Itoh, social worker who worked for the International Social Service in the 1950s and 1960s in Kure, was interviewed by the author in 1994 and 1995 in Tokyo. She put her effort into establishing welfare and scholarship funds for the mixed-blood children who had financial problems. With substantial assistance from the Ferguson Fund which was established in 1964 in Australia, the service assisted many children to continue their education and establish their careers.

15 On the history of Japanese migration to Australia, see Hunt, 1986; Nagata, 1996; Sissons, 1972, 1977a, 1977b, 1988.

16 On Japanese internment in Australia, see Bevege, 1993; Nagata, 1987, 1989, 1990, 1996; Zainu'ddin, 1985.

17 W.D. Borrie's figure quoted in Lack and Templeton, 1995: 44.

18 Australian Consulate General, Geneva, "Report on Minorities Article, 6 May 1953", quoted in Ann-Mari Jordens, 1995: 9–10.

19 Quoted in Lack and Templeton, 1995: 14.

20 Pickled cucumber with *ochazuke* is a dish many Japanese enjoy after eating rich food.

21 *Shufu no tomo* is a Japanese journal started as a monthly magazine for housewives in 1927 and became the top-selling magazine in three years. Before the war, monthly sales of *Shufu no tomo* reached 1.6 million. The magazine has continued its publication up to the present.

22 Sōka Gakkai which was founded in 1930 is the largest new religion in Japan. It is an independent lay organisation of the Buddhist sect Nichiren Shōshū. Its chief temple is Taisekiji, in Shizuoka Prefecture. The number of followers counts 17 million in Japan (1985) and 1.26 million overseas (1989).

23 These sentences were from Michi's essay which was circulated among her family privately around 1990.

24 The current (2000) exchange rate is about 66 yen to a dollar. In 1996, the Australian dollar went as low as 60 yen to a dollar.

25 An inquest was held into his death, but nothing became clearer for Michi. She did not talk about this issue much.

26 Condolence money at the funeral is called *kōden* in Japanese and it is customary to give some money as respect for the dead.

27 When I interviewed Michi in 1995, she was wondering whether she should let Gus return to her or not after he begged to be forgiven. I understood they occasionally saw each other without the children's knowledge.

28 There were several American novels and films which depicted relationships between Japanese women and American men and some of them were popular in the 1950s in the United States as well as in Australia. A film titled *Japanese War Bride* was made in 1952 in America. James Michener's novel *Sayonara* was a bestseller and made into a film in 1957. Similarly, a 1956 film which was based on Vern Sneider's novel *The Teahouse of the August Moon* attracted an audience.

Selected References

Bevege, Margaret
1993 *Behind Barbed Wire: Internment in Australia During World War II*. St Lucia: University of Queensland Press.

Blair, Teruko
1991 *Ōsutoraria ni idakarete [Embraced by Australia]*. Tokyo: TV Asahi.

Carter, Isobel Ray
1965 *Alien Blossom: A Japanese-Australian Love Story*. Melbourne: Lansdowne Press.

Chida, Takeshi
1997 *Eirenpōgun no nihon shinchū to tenkai*. Tokyo: Ochanomizu shobō.

Endō, Masako
1989 *Cheri Pākā no atsui fuyu [Warbride: A Long Way to Australia]*. Tokyo: Shinchōsha.

Hunt, Suzan Jane
1986 *Spinifex and Hessian: Women's Lives in North-Western Australia 1860–1900*. Nedlands, WA: University of Western Australia Press.

Jordens, Ann-Mari
1995 *Redefining Australians: Immigration, Citizenship and National Identity*. Sydney: Hale and Iremonger.

Kureshishi-hensan-iinkai (ed.)
1995 *Kure shishi*. Kure: Kure City Office.

Kureshishi-hensanshitsu
1996 *Kure no ayumi II [History of Kure 2]* Kure: Kure City Office.

Selected references

Lack, John, and Jacqueline Templeton
1995 *Bold Experiment: A Documentary History of Australian Immigration since 1945*. Melbourne: Oxford University Press.

Nagata, Yuriko
1987 Japanese Internees at Loveday, 1941–1946. *Journal of the Historical Society of South Australia*, (15): 65–81.

Nagata, Yuriko
1989 Repatriating Japanese Internees. *Journal of the Australian War Memorial*, (15): 15–25.

Nagata, Yuriko
1990 A Foot in the Door: Japanese Immgration to Australia after WWII (1946–1952). The National Conference of the Asian Studies Association of Australia, Griffith University, 1990.

Nagata, Yuriko
1996 *Unwanted Aliens: Japanese Internment in Australia*. St Lucia: University of Queensland Press.

Sissons, David C.S.
1972 Immigration in Australia-Japanese Relations. In: J. Stockwin (ed.), *Japan and Australia in the Seventies*. Sydney: Angus and Robertson.

Sissons, David C.S.
1977a Karayuki-san: Japanese Prostitutes in Australia 1887–1916, Part 1. *Historical Studies*, 17(68): 323–341.

Sissons, David C.S.
1977b Karayuki-san: Japanese Prostitutes in Australia 1887–1916, Part 2. *Historical Studies*, 17(69): 474–488.

Sissons, David C.S.
1988 Japanese. In: James Jupp (ed.), *The Australian People: An Encyclopedia of the Nation, its People and their Origins*; pp. 635–637. North Ryde, NSW: Angus and Robertson.

Tamura, Keiko
1997 Border Crossings: Changing Identities of Japanese War Brides. *The Asia–Pacific Magazine*: 43–47.

Selected references

Tamura, Keiko
1998 Sensō hanayome no ōsutoraria. In Japan Club of Australia (ed.), *Ōsutoraria no nihonjin*. Sydney: Japan Club of Australia.

Tamura, Keiko
1999 Border Crossings: Japanese War Brides and their Selfhood. [Unpublished PhD thesis], The Australian National University.

Zainu'ddin, Alisa G. Thomson
1985 Rose Inagaki: Is it a Crime to Marry a Foreigner? In F. Kelly and M. Lake (eds), *Double Time: Women in Victoria's 150 Years*. Ringwood, Vic.: Penguin Books.

About the Author

Keiko Tamura was born and raised in Osaka, Japan. After graduating in English from Kobe College, she moved to Canberra to carry out her postgraduate studies in anthropology. She was awarded a PhD degree from the Australian National University in 2000 with a thesis titled, "Border Crossings: Japanese War Brides and their Selfhood". As well as working as a freelance interpreter, she was a Senior Research Officer in the Australia–Japan Research Project at the Australian War Memorial from 1997 to 1998 and held a Postdoctoral Fellowship in the Research School of Pacific and Asian Studies at the Australian National University from 2000 to 2001. Her academic interests range widely and include Aboriginal Australia, Australia–Japan relations, migration and women's experience of war. She lives with her British husband, and two sons, one Australian-born and the other German-born, in Canberra.

www.ingramcontent.com/pod-product-compliance
Lightning Source LLC
Chambersburg PA
CBHW040320170426
43192CB00030B/2841